Table of Content

Map of Kenya	2
Introduction	3
Main findings	5
Glossary	11

SECTION ONE

Introduction	12
Objectives	12
Research method	12
Data collection and sampling	12
Respondents to the survey	13
Respondents' competence in Arabic	14
Research challenges	15

SECTION TWO

Islam and Muslims	16
Main Muslim groups	17
Muslim ideological communities	18
Muslim religious practice	19
Mihadhara	22
Darsa	23

SECTION THREE

Mosque construction	25
Distribution of mosques in the Provinces	26
Distribution of mosques in the Districts	27
Registration of mosques	27
Mosque sponsorship, leadership and organization	28
Mosque finances	30
Disputes at the mosques	32

SECTION FOUR

Imams	36
Imams' madrasa education	37
Khutba and policy	39
Imams and politics in the mosques	40
Imams and socio-political issues	42
Addressing terrorism	43
Imams' networks	44

SECTION FIVE

Muslims and politics	46
Muslims and freedom of worship	47
Idea of an Islamic political party	51
Mosques, politicians and political leadership	52
Muslim organizations	54
SUPKEM	55
Council of Imams and Preachers of Islam in Kenya (CIPK)	57
Muslim media	58
The Friday Bulletin	60
Muslim women	61
Social services	65
Access to madrasa	67
Credit facilities	67
Youth in the mosque	69

SECTION SIX

Kadhi courts	70
Muslims and the West	72

SECTION SEVEN

Muslim perspectives on economy and development	74
Muslim priorities for development	76

CASE STUDIES

Mosques in Nakuru	78
Mosques in Kisumu	80
Mosque in Mumias	81
Tanwir Da'awa Women's Group, Nakuru	83
Conflicts at Mlango wa Papa Mosque	83
Bibliography	84

Map of Kenya showing regions of Muslim concentration

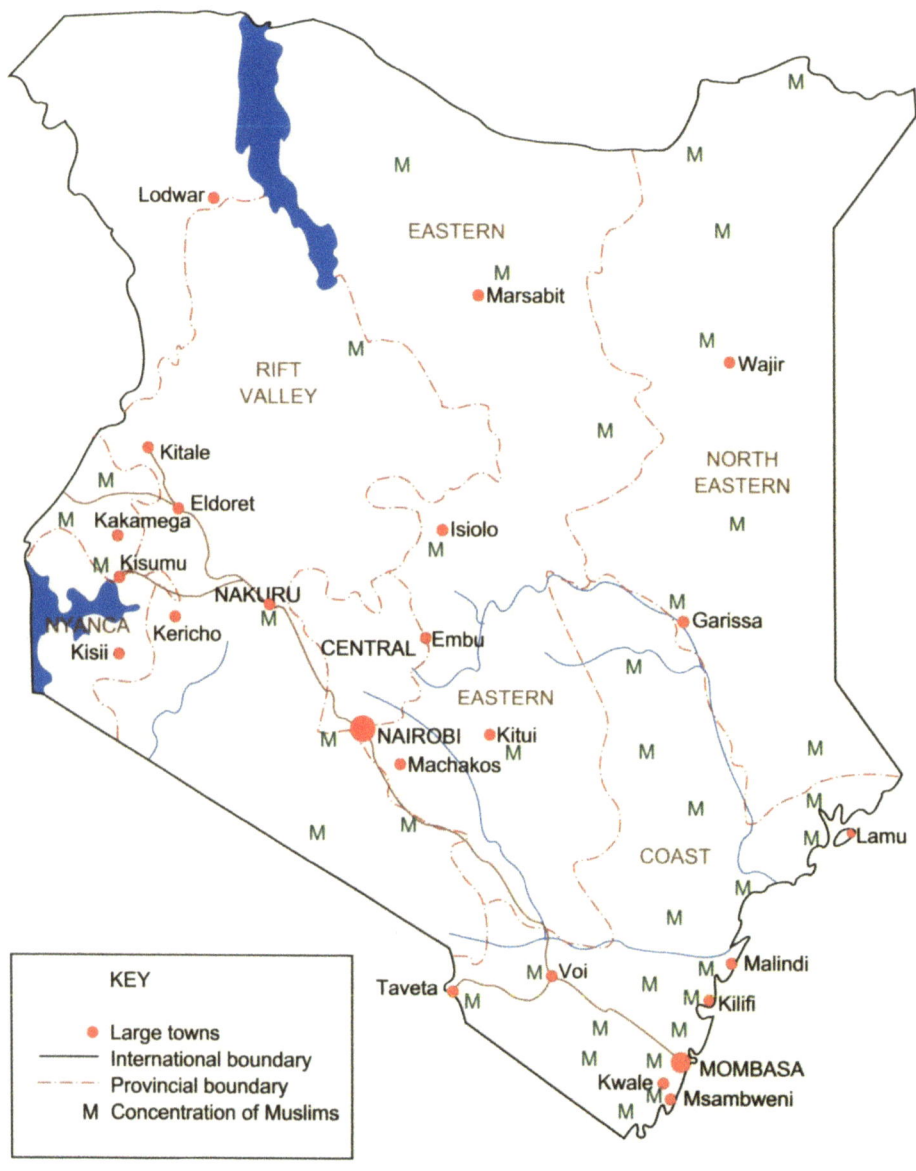

Introduction

Islam has a number of social institutions (e.g. mosques, *madrasa*) which provide for the religious needs of the communities. The mosque is one such institution that could encompass religious, social, economic and political functions. Muslims consider the mosque to be symbolically an important house of prayer (*salat*) but also an environment in which varied dispositions of the lives of Muslim communities are reflected.

In Kenya mosques facilitate worship and actualize Muslim lives. In the practice of prayer the mosque has double roles, either as a prayer house or facilitates the congregational weekly prayer (*jumaah salat*) on Fridays. Whether a mosque is big or small, either richly endowed or with meager resources, holding the *jumaah salat* or not usually reflects on the communal discourse in particular the status of the practice of Islam in the mosque environment.

This report projects the mosque as an institution capable of playing a unique and vital role of directing Muslim opinions and compensate for the absence of strong supporting civic institutions amongst Muslims in Kenya. This unique portrayal of the centrality of the opinions of mosque participants is important and essential for Muslim leaders, policy makers and the public.

An understanding of the opinion and roles played by mosque participants is a significant consideration in efforts to steer and nurture a progressive Muslim community. On the basis of the role and position of the mosque in Kenya, this report presents statistical factual details to assist in understanding a hitherto little understood Muslim community in Kenya.

The survey on which its results are presented here was conceptualized to provide historical and contemporary perspectives on Muslim lives because despite the presence of Islam for centuries in some parts of Kenya there is still inadequate comprehensive and contemporary data on various aspects of Muslim communities and institutions. This inadequacy provoked my curiosity and created the interest in me to conduct an empirical survey on various aspects of Muslim lives but central based on the institutions of the mosque. The study was also conducted as an attempt to comprehend contemporary developments in the relationship between Muslims and the wider society in Kenya and globally because until the tragic events of terrorist attacks on the American Embassy in 1998 the public faces of Islam in Kenya was largely confined to matters of spirituality and rituals. However, the consequence of that one event has meant government officials and the Kenyan public both Muslim and non-Muslim has become increasingly interested in what is happening in the Muslim community. Subsequently Muslims feel they have been placed under a microscope by the government and state agents. For example the government attempt to undertake a study of the *madrasa* in Kenya in response to claims that *madrasa* teach elements that encouraged terrorism. This attempt to 'extract data' was rebuffed by the Muslim community and ended in failure. Since then research activity happen to be misunderstood in the Muslim community and there is always scant information on Islam and Muslim institutions in Kenya. Whenever a need for data and information on aspects of Islam and Muslim lives in Kenya emerges 'experts' are left scratching their heads in attempt to distinguish between facts, urban legend and fiction about Islam and Muslim in Kenya.

The results presented in this report are from an effort involving the participation of members of the Muslim community in providing baseline data on the role of the mosques in understanding and pointing to details of Muslim history, politics, religion and development. The mosque was picked as a focus institution from which its participants were encouraged to articulate opinions and ideas towards the creation of a body of knowledge for continuous study and reference points.

The results presented in this report are comprehensive findings of the opinions of mosque participants collected from a mosque based survey comprising 'mosque goers' from sixteen districts in eight provinces of Kenya. Based on filled-up questionnaire and follow-up in-depth interviews with selected members of the Muslim communities, statistical overview are presented through graphs aimed at providing an assessment of Muslim opinions about their institutions, strengths, worries and concerns.

This survey and the statistical method was chosen on the premise that Muslims in Kenya must address, debate and contribute to pressing issues facing the society and nation based on rigorous data and information. I believe then, before undertaking the survey and now that the results are out that optimal analysis and treatment of social issues demands a comprehensive and continuous evaluation from several diverse approaches. While social challenges are becoming more complex and interwoven incorporating new voices and adding diversity to the realm of ideas and knowledge and how to get to it should be the norm rather than exception. I hope that the results of this survey will generate a new and more creative approach if not an alternative perspective to addressing societal matters involving Muslims in Kenya and other African countries.

The fieldwork research that enabled me to proceed with this project was made possible through an initial grant from the Andrew W. Mellow Foundation Small Grant Project through the Universities Science and Humanities Partnerships in Africa (Ushepia) at the University of Cape Town, South Africa. I would like to thank my host institution in Berlin, the Zentrum Moderner Orient, (ZMO) and the Deutsche Forschungsgemeinschaft (DFG) for a subsidy towards the publication of this report.

This survey could not have been conducted were it not for the efforts of my research assistants. I would like to thank Kadara Swaleh, Hamisi Mtityo, Abdalla Mwakutwaa and Chembeya for their enthusiasm in the data collection, interviews, data entry and analysis. Lina Falkenberg, my student assistant at the ZMO assisted in various ways in the process of producing this report. I thank also Prof Ian Linden who made very useful comments from the very beginning of the survey and read and corrected parts of the draft. I prepared this report while resident at the Zentrum Moderner Orient, Berlin, Germany which provided an academic ambience and peaceful atmosphere to reflect on the possible varieties of meanings of the statistical details. All errors arising from the interpretation and presentation of the results of the survey are entirely of my own.

Hassan Mwakimako PhD
July 2007
Berlin, Germany

Main findings

Islam has spread to most areas of Kenya but is mainly concentrated on the Coast and North Eastern Province. Islam has also spread in other areas creating a significant concentration of Muslims in major cities, towns and urban areas. The Muslim population is a diverse and heterogeneous population of distinctive cultural groupings, ethnic identities, racial and sectarian traits.

The Muslim segments of the population feel and to some extent may well be, marginalized and discriminated against as Muslims and as inhabitants of particular regions or as members of certain disadvantaged ethnic communities.

Amongst the segmented Muslim communities, the Asian communities appears best organized and most prosperous, but the majority of indigenous Muslims live in conditions of poverty with meager resources. African Muslims are stacked at the 'bottom of the barrel' with no community programs geared to addressing poverty and underdevelopment.

The highlighted figures below present the most profound findings of the study. In most of the cases the statistical figures will not tally to one hundred percent, such completed results are discussed in the main text of the report.

Education

A large number of Muslims remain largely uneducated or poorly educated. Imams, the leaders of Muslim opinion are generally people of low education in Islamic religious sciences and learning. Lack of advanced religious knowledge by a majority of Muslim leaders and limited exposure to secular learning by many Imams means Muslim knowledge remains archaic, Islamic institution inadequately modernized, with the mosque remaining only a place of prayer and sectarian controversy.

Levels of formal school (secular) education attained by Imams are generally low. Forty eight percent (48%) of Imams have not benefited from formal secular education. Eighteen percent (18%) of Imams have primary levels of secular education; twenty two percent (22%) have secondary levels of secular education; ten percent (10%) of Imams indicated to have a college certificate (not university); two percent (2%) have university level of secular education.

Levels of *madrasa* education attained by most Imams are surprisingly low. Thirty eight percent (38%) of Imams had *mutawwasit* levels (mid-level), twelve percent (12%) were *ibtidai* (secondary level), twenty six percent (26%) had *thanawi* (post-secondary not university), and twelve percent (12%) of Imams had *jamiah* (university) levels. Thirteen percent (12%) of Imams received informal religious instructions and knowledge from prominent *ulama* outside formalized institutions (*halaqa*).

Madrasa

Muslims have an easy access to the *madrasa*. Seventy eight percent (78%) of the sample felt they had easy access to the *madrasa*, thirteen percent (13%) said it was difficult; nine percent (9%) found it extremely difficult to access a *madrasa*.

In the provinces, the Coast Province experience the highest demand for *madrasa* education. Sixty five percent (65%) of Muslims in the Coast Province said the *madrasa* were not adequate and faced difficulties in getting to *madrasa*.

Muslims have fair command of Arabic language. Thirty five percent (35%) of Muslims had excellent command of Arabic, twenty two percent (22%) had a good command, and fifteen percent (15%) fairly understood Arabic while twenty eight percent (28%) either had bad or poor command of the Arabic language.

Mosques

Fifty two percent (52%) were constructed and sponsored by local communities; twenty percent (20%) are constructed and are under the management of foreign organizations.

Sixty eight percent (68%) of mosques do not have constitutions. Fifty seven percent (57%) of mosques without constitutions are in the Coast Province.

Eighty percent (80%) of mosques were managed by a committee; forty seven percent (47%) of mosques did not hold elections for the mosque committee.

Most mosques were registered with a government law. Forty three percent (43%) are registered as *wakf* (religious endowments), twenty nine percent (29%) are registered as societies, five percent (5%) are under a government department (prisons etc); about fifteen percent (15%) of mosques are not registered.

The majority of *ratibs* who attend prayers at mosques are not registered with the mosques. Lack of official registration at mosques means that *ratibs* may not always have legal rights in what happens at the mosques.

Intra-factional disputes and theological controversies take up a lot of energy. Sixty two percent (62%) of mosques have experience serious conflicts over ideological matters and religious practice.

Mosques finances

The majority of mosques in Kenya face very serious financial difficulties. Sixty five percent (65%) of mosques were experiencing serious financial difficulties, twenty percent (20%) were in a good financial position, and five percent (5%) were enjoying an excellent financial position.

During the last five years (from 2000) twenty percent (20%) of mosques have experienced a worsening financial position, thirty eight percent (38%) have remained in the same financial position while thirty two percent (32%) have indicated an improvement in their financial position.

Islamic finance is a new phenomenon in Kenya introduced in mid 2006 through conventional banks. Before then seventy two percent (72%) of Muslims had serious difficulties to get credit, twenty percent (20%) had not attempted to get credit; five percent (5%) of Muslims had easy access to getting credit in Kenya. Forty eight percent (48%) of Muslims with difficulties in getting credit are from the Coast Province.

The majority of Muslims did not approach conventional banks for credit because they were concerned about being charged interest. Because conventional banking had not yet started to offer *sharia* compliant services most Muslims kept away from borrowing from such institutions. There were attempts to establish *sharia* compliant banks during the period of the survey.

Mosque khutba and policy

Fifty five percent (55%) of Imams in the mosques are in regular employment receiving a salary from mosque resources.

Muslims indicated that the dangers of terrorism are not adequately discussed in the *khutba*, forty percent (40%) of Muslims said Imams did not at all discuss the dangers of terrorism, forty five percent (45%) of Muslims indicated that Imams discussed dangers of terrorism but 'just a little', ten percent (10%) of Muslims said Imams discussed 'a lot' about the dangers of terrorism.

However, in most cases terrorism was mentioned in the *khutba* in responses to, or as complains about the arbitrary arrests of Muslims suspected of involvement in acts of terrorism.

Twenty percent (20%) of Muslims in Kenya said freedom of worship was worse in 2006 compared to 2005. Thirty eight percent (38%) of Muslims did not notice any improvement in the conditions of freedom of worship in 2006 compared to 2005. Nine percent (9%) of Muslims said conditions of freedom of worship had improved in 2006 compared to 2005. The rest thirty seven percent (37%) did not have any opinion on this aspect of the survey.

Fifty five percent (55%) of Muslims in North Eastern Province said freedom of worship has worsened in Kenya.

Fifty five percent (55%) of Muslims in Coast Province thought conditions of freedom of worship had improved in Kenya.

Politics

The Muslim people of Kenya are at a political and social crossroads; they have undergone massive political shifts, and become a relevant part of the political landscape in Kenya. Muslims are a politically active group. A high proportion participates actively in community affairs and 'political horserace' questions are particularly interesting to them. Muslims intend to be part of the political system and consider it important for them to participate in politics.

Forty three percent (43%) said they were keen and very interested in public affairs, twenty six percent (26%) of Muslims said they were keen but not active in public affairs.

Muslims in Coast Province were skeptical about participating in public affairs; sixty percent (60%) would not attend public gatherings (*baraza*).

Fifty percent (50%) of Muslims discuss politics with friends and family. Thirty five percent (35%) occasionally engaged friends and family in political discussions, ten percent (10%) hardly engaged in politics with friends and family.

Fifty nine percent (59%) of Muslims in Coast Province do not discuss politics with family and friends.

Seventy five percent (75%) of Muslims prefer the establishments of a Muslim political party, ten percent (10%) are not in favor of a Muslim political party, five percent (5%) were undecided.

Muslims prefer to participate actively in national politics. Fifty five percent (55%) of Muslims strongly agreed that it is a religious duty for Muslims to take part in politics, twenty eight percent (28%) 'just agreed'.

Fifteen percent (15%) of Muslims are not in favor of Muslims participating in politics in Kenya because the affairs of the state are not run in accordance to Islamic norms. Fifty five percent (55%) of Muslims accused the government of meddling and interfering in Muslim affairs.

Muslims face lack of unity in Kenya. Fifty six percent (56%) of Muslims 'strongly agreed' that lack of Muslim unity was worrying, thirty seven percent (37%) were 'worried' by lack of Muslim unity; five percent (5%) did not think that Kenya Muslims were not united.

Muslims lowly rate the ability in parliament to articulate in unison Muslim concerns is notable. Muslim politicians do not have strong links to mosques in Kenya. Seventy percent (70%) of mosques had never been visited by a politician.

Sixty percent (60%) of Muslims were strongly concerned over fewer appointments of Muslims to high offices in the government. Five percent (5%) thought the government has done enough while another five percent (5%) held a neutral position on this concern.

Media

In December 2006, Muslims had established at least three FM radio stations in Kenya. However, few Muslims get their news from 'Islamic Radio' networks. Forty seven percent (47%) of Muslims do not at all get news through a Muslim radio station. Forty two percent (42%) listened to news from Islamic radio only a 'few times a week'.

Fifty eight percent (58%) of Muslims in the Coast Province did not listen to news from a Muslim radio station. The majority of Muslims in Nyanza, Western and Rift Valley Provinces 'never listen' to news from an Islamic radio station. This is because these provinces were not served by Islamic radio during the survey period.

Television is the most popular source of news amongst Muslims. Forty percent (40%) watched news on television daily. Thirty five percent (35%) watched news from television regularly, yet twenty percent (20%) of Muslims did not have access to a television set.

There is no Muslim daily newspaper in Kenya although Muslims produce pamphlets once in a while. In the 1990's the Islamic Party of Kenya (IPK) published the 'Milestone' to articulate a Muslim position on politics; it has however become moribund. The 'Friday Bulletin' is the most widely read Muslim publication. Seventy five percent (75%) of Muslims read the 'Friday Bulletin'. But its circulation is limited to Nairobi and Central Kenya. The 'Friday Bulletin' does not have a wide circulation amongst Muslims in the Coast and North Eastern Provinces.

Muslim women

Generally, Kenyan Muslim woman appears unfairly treated, molested, and at best treated as an inferior partner in decision making. This state of affairs is promoted by biased feelings and overzealous interpretations of the authority of religious texts on polygamous marriages, inheritance and divorce.

At the mosque, Muslim women perceive themselves as being unduly disadvantaged. A fundamental problem does in fact exist in that Muslim woman like all Kenyan women are disadvantaged when it comes to education, incomes, wealth distribution, land ownership but women's role in the society is not considered an issue in Muslim communities.

Muslim women are not adequately represented in leadership. Eighty percent (80%) of mosque committees did not include women participants. Sixty five percent (65%) of Muslim men disapproved and will not support women's participation in the mosque committee. Seventy six percent (76%) of mosques did not invite women to participate in recent seminars held at the mosques.

Seventy two percent (72%) of Muslim would not support the election of women to parliament. But fifty percent (50%) of Muslims in the Coast Province will support the election of Muslim women to political office. Generally the status of the Muslim woman requires immediate redress.

Religious practices

The majority of Muslims in Kenya are Sunni with small pockets of Shiite. Most Shiite belong to the Ithna-ashari and Bohra communities.

In the 1960-1970s the practice of Islam manifested itself through ritualistic practice and ceremonies. The *mawlid* and *dhikr* were popular. However, from the 1990's Muslims have been influenced by highly contested ideologies like Wahabism which opposed *dhikr* and *mawlid* ceremonies

Mawlid celebrations are popular in Kenya so is the opposition to its practice. Forty eight percent (48%) of Muslims often attend *mawlid*, forty three percent (43%) are opposed to the *mawlid* and will 'never' attend them, and about five percent (5%) have attended at *mawlid* perhaps 'once' or 'twice.'

Forty two percent (42%) of Muslims do not attend *dhikr*, twenty eight percent (28%) will occasionally attend while thirty percent (30%) 'always' attend *dhikr*.

Most mosques are involved in outreach programs in the community. *Da'awa* is the most popular outreach activity. Seventy percent (70%) of mosques have hosted a visiting *da'awa* group.

Mihadhara (public preaching sessions) are popular with Muslims. Sixty one percent (61%) of Muslims will always attend *mihadhara*, twenty three percent (23%) occasional attend; eight percent (8%) never attends *mihadhara*.

Mihadhara are most popular in North Eastern Province. Sixty eight percent (68%) of Muslims who do not attend *mihadhara* are in the Coast Province.

Darsa (mosque lectures) are popular amongst Muslims in Kenya. Eighty two percent (82%) of Muslims always attend *darsa*, five percent (5%) never attend *darsa*.

Muslim organization

Sixty three percent (63%) of Muslims thought Muslim organizations are not managed in democratic manner. Thirty percent (30%) thought this situation will prevail in the future.

Twenty five percent (25%) of Muslims did not trust the leadership of Supreme Council of Kenya Muslims (SUPKEM), forty five percent (45%) had 'just a little' trust in the leadership of SUPKEM, fifteen percent (15%) had a lot of confidence and trust in the leadership of SUPKEM, five percent (5%) of Muslims have 'not heard' of the existence of SUPKEM, and five percent (5%) of Muslims 'somewhat' trust the leadership of SUPKEM.

Most Muslims are skeptical about the leadership claims by Council of Imams and Preachers of Islam in Kenya (CIPK). The majority of Muslims have little confidence in CIPK, twenty eight percent (28%) of Muslim do 'not at all' trust CIPK leadership, twenty five percent (25%) had 'just a little' confidence in the leadership of CIPK, twenty percent (20%) have 'not heard' about the existence of CIPK, twenty percent (20%) of Muslims had a 'lot of trust' and confidence in the leadership of CIPK.

Muslims and the state

Kadhi courts are popular with Muslims. Seventy five percent (75%) of Muslims had friends and family who had visited the *kadhi* courts during 2005.

Sixty eight percent (68%) of Muslims consider the *kadhi* court a constitutional right not a privilege.

Twenty percent (20%) of Muslims did not know who employs the Chief Kadhi, sixteen percent (16%) thought the Chief Kadhi was employed by a Muslim organization; fifty eight percent (58%) of Muslims were sure and confident that the Chief Kadhi was not employed by a Muslim organization.

Twenty six percent (26%) of Muslims feel supporting the government will be reciprocated with government support for the *kadhi* court.

Seventy five percent (75%) of Muslims do not want people of other religions to decide on the fate of the *kadhi* courts in the Constitution, twenty percent (20%) thought people of other religions should be included in the matter, five percent (5%) did not know what to do about it.

Social amenities

Muslims lack access to social amenities like libraries, social hall, and medical services. Sixty eight percent (68%) of Muslims said it was 'very difficult' to access a library. Ten percent (10%) of Muslims do not make any effort to look for a library; fifteen percent (15%) of Muslims had easy access to a library.

Sixty percent (60%) of Muslims in the Coast Province experienced difficulties in finding a library. Fifty two percent of Muslims in Nyanza and Rift Valley had easy access to a library.

Thirty eight percent (38%) of Muslims faced extreme difficulty in getting access to medical facilities, while thirty five percent (35%) of Muslims said it is difficult to access a medical facility. Fifty five percent (55%) of Muslims in the Coast Province faced extreme difficulty in getting access to medical facilities.

Lack of essential social facilities, poor health, inadequate schools, poor access to credit means extra effort is needed to address societal imbalances prevalent amongst Muslims in Kenya.

Muslims expectations

Muslim areas are severely underdeveloped; levels of education and availability of health services are overstretched in the Coast and North Eastern Province (home to an exclusive Muslim grouping). However, finding credible partners to realize development amongst Muslims societies remain the greatest challenges for the majority of Muslims in the Coast and North Eastern Province.

More and more Muslims realize the importance and significance of education, there is concern to address job creation, reduce poverty and eradicate drug abuse.

In a rating of seven areas of significance and priorities for development, thirty percent (30%) of Muslims mentioned education as the highest priority, sixteen percent (16%) mentioned political participation, sixteen percent (16%), Muslim unity, fourteen percent (14%) mentioned tackling poverty, twelve percent (12%) mentioned unemployment, ten percent (10%) mentioned both health and drugs while family counseling accounted four percent (4%).

In order to enhance development Muslims in the Coast Province had the following preferences; economic empowerment and unemployment, thirty eight percent (38%), education, twenty two percent (22%), political participation, fifteen percent (15%), health and drug abuse, fifteen percent (15%), good leadership and Muslim unity, ten percent (10%); fight against terrorism, two percent (2%).

Muslims in North Eastern Province prioritize the following to enhance development; economic empowerment, unemployment and poverty alleviation, thirty eight percent (38%); politics, twenty percent (20%); education, twenty percent (20%); health and drug abuse, sixteen percent (16%); religious consciousness (3%); peace building (3%).

Glossary

Adhan	the call for prayer from the mosque during the five obligatory prayer times
Ahl al Sunna	people who follow the way of life of the Prophet Muhammad
Akidah	a way in which people of communities practice Islam
Alim	a scholar, one with knowledge
Baraza	a meeting place usually in open court yards or ground, a political meeting addressed by local leaders
Bid'a	an innovation in the religion of Islam
CIPK	Council of Imams and Preachers of Islam in Kenya
Da'awa	an act of propagating Islam
Darsa	lectures usually given at the mosque
Dhikr	a ritualistic continuous invocation of the name of Allah as a form of prayer
Dua	supplication
Eid-ul Adha	celebration after the completion of the *hajj*, festival of the sacrifice
Eid ul Fitr	celebration after the end of the fast of Ramadan
Fajr	early morning prayer
Fi-sabillillah	for the cause of Allah
Halaqa	a system of learning where one becomes a student or protégé of a scholar
IIRO	International Islamic Relief Organization
Imam	a person who lead others during (prayer) salat
IPK	Islamic Party of Kenya
Jamiah	university level of education
Jumaah	friday, afternoon prayer on the friday
KAULI	Kenya Assembly of Ulama in Islam
Khutba	a sermon
Madrasa	institution where the Qu'ran and other forms of Islamic knowledge is taught
Markaz	usually an annual meeting, events involving da'awa groups
Mawlid	celebration marking the birth of Prophet Muhammad
Mihadhara	open ground public preaching of Islam
MP	Member of Parliament
NUKEM	National Union of Kenya Muslims
Qira'ah	recitation of the Qu'ran based on the correct pronunciation
Qunut	supplications offered after in response to calamity
Ramadan	ninth month of the Islamic lunar calendar when Muslims are expected to observe the fast
Ratib	one who regularly prayers at a particular mosque
Ra'y	independent opinion
Salat	prayer
SUPKEM	Supreme Council of Kenya Muslims
Tabligh	a group (action) of missionaries who travel together preaching Islam
Taqlid	practice of blind following of religious practice and teachings
Ummah	the Muslim community
Wahhabi	Islamic teachings associated with an 18th century scholar Muhammad Ibn Abdul Wahhab
Wakf	pious endowments
YMA	Young Muslims Association
Ziyara	visit to the tombs for veneration

SECTION ONE

Introduction

The story of Islam in Kenya is a long and checkered one. Suffice to say Islam and Muslims in Kenya are receiving a great deal of attention from international press, scholars and social commentators. Government officials and the Kenyan public too have become increasingly interested in the Muslim community thereby placing Muslims under a microscope. Yet, little is known about Muslims in Kenya and far less about the activities and views of its adherents. This need can only be achieved successfully through in-depth empirical research on the Muslim communities. It is with this goal in mind that this study on the mosques and Muslim views in Kenya was conducted.

This public opinion survey amongst Muslims in Kenya encompasses a broad array of subjects ranging from people's assessments of their own lives to their views about the current state of global and local politics. This report provides a wealth of statistics and a penetrating first glimpse into the Muslim community of Kenya. It presents information on aspects of Muslim demographic diversities, Muslim views on policy, and interaction with the state, politics, religion, social and economic developments, availability of resources and the existing potential.

Objectives

- To determine the extent of the Muslim populations in Kenya and determine their main needs as voiced by Muslims themselves.
- Give a general profile of Muslims in Kenya, reflecting their religious characteristics, social facilities and services available to them.
- Suggest long term goals for Muslims in Kenya.
- Act as a basis for further research into the welfare of Muslims in Kenya.

Research method

The geographical areas selected for this study covered sixteen districts from eight administrative provinces in Kenya. This selection was based on the following criteria:
- Geographical coverage;
- Availability of Muslim institutions and Muslim communities;
- Cultural diversity (Muslims of Arab, African, Swahili origins);
- Rural/urban dichotomy;
- Convenience of access, rapport with Muslim leaders and security concerns based on experiences from previous research amongst Muslims.

Data collection and sampling

The study elicited data primary from survey interviews and focused group discussions (FGD). The first was based on a semi-structured questionnaire and the later on a FGD guide. The interviews and FGD were conducted in English and Kiswahili. Within the context of the survey interviews the study also carried out in depth interviews with key informants.

The use of existing information, open-ended interviews, closed focus surveys and field observation were the main research tools employed. Background data on Muslims' living conditions was collected during February-March 2006. In April-August field work was carried out covering a total of sixteen districts from eight administrative provinces in Kenya. The areas were selected randomly but comprise regions with majority Muslims while others have significant minority Muslim populations. The purpose was to gather information on Muslims thinking on a variety of social, religious, economic and political matters affecting the Muslims peoples and the population of Kenya in general.

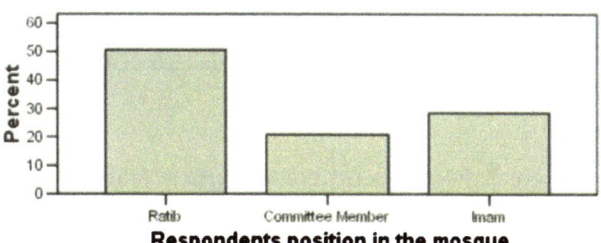

Fig. 1: Respondents position in the mosques

All respondents to the questionnaire were Muslims who identified themselves as members of particular mosque and that they were participants not just in prayers but other mosque activities. Participants in this survey were at least 18 years old and responded to the survey questionnaire voluntarily.

The sample for this study was drawn carefully as Muslims do not reside everywhere in the selected research areas. Overall 1311 interview questionnaires were randomly selected and included in the survey. The questionnaire comprised responses from *ratibs* from a total of 103 mosques spread in the areas covered by the survey. The interviews with mosque attendees are used in this survey to complement the statistical overviews and assessments. The results of the definitive data from which a comprehensive narrative report is presented was tabulated using SPSS. In some cases where the percentages will not tally to one hundred percent its because we have left out some aspects of the analysis which appear insignificant or not relevant to be highlighted on this report.

Respondents to the survey

The survey gathered data centered on the Mosque and its participants. Three categories of mosque congregation were asked to respond to a prepared questionnaire. These included; *ratibs*, Imams and committee members.

The respondents were selected because their affiliation to the mosques was based on their partaking of worship at the mosque and participating in other activities associated with the mosque. The majority of participants selected in this survey were *ratibs*, the ordinary people who worshipped at the mosques but did not hold positions of leadership. *Ratibs* accounted for fifty six percent (56%) of respondents. Imams, the leaders of prayers amongst Sunni Muslims comprised twenty five percent (25%) of respondents. Nineteen percent (19%) are mosque participants holding positions of leadership in the mosque committee.

Muslims identified with a particular mosque because they attended regular prayers in them not because they had voluntarily registered their membership by signing a membership form or paying annual dues and subscriptions.

The survey found that the majority of respondents were *ratibs* of mosques but only a few had signed membership forms. Between ten to eighteen percent (10%-18%) of mosques had no records of *ratibs* nor signed registration forms. Eighty two percent (82%) of mosques did not have their *ratibs* registered with the mosques. Mosques neither required *ratibs* to register nor kept a record of membership. This trend has some negative effects on mosque stability. Lack of legal identification with a particular mosque means that Mus-

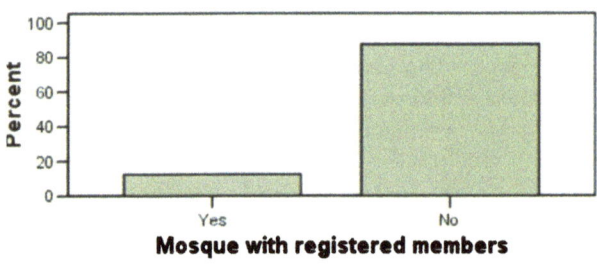

Fig. 2: Mosques with registered membership

lims are not duty bound to participate in mosque activity. In many mosques interviewees pointed to this trend as responsible for weak leadership of mosques committee and lack of commitment by most Muslims to improve the conditions of mosque. It was suggested in subsequent discussions that mosques should be encouraged to keep lists of membership and call upon such members to dedicate themselves to assist the mosque financially through annual or periodical subscriptions.

Respondents' competence in Arabic

The survey captured the respondents' competence in Arabic language based on the strength and importance of Arabic as a lingua franca of the Muslim prayer (*salat*) and sermon (*khutba*). The survey brought in results ranging from respondents claiming to have an excellent command of Arabic to those completely unfamiliar with the Arabic language. Thirty two percent (32%) of respondents thought they had an excellent command of Arabic. Some twenty two percent (22%) said their command of Arabic was good, while fifteen percent (15%) considered they had a fair comprehension of Arabic.

Muslims whose knowledge of Arabic fell between fairly bad and poor command accounted for thirty percent (30%) of the respondents. Competence in Arabic can be used to measures how much Muslims are able to understand the Qu'ran on their own and how much of the population depends on others to read and understand the basic texts of Muslim religion.

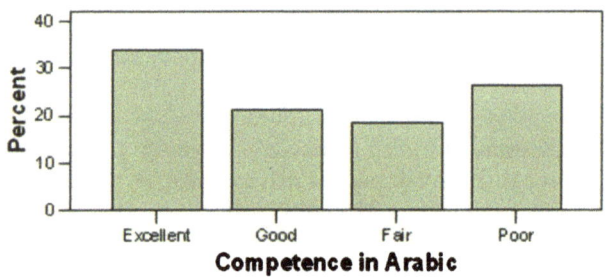

Fig. 3: Respondents' competence in Arabic

Although Kiswahili is the main language spoken amongst Muslims in Kenya, Arabic is always used in the *khutba* and most of religious speech is legitimized with interposed Arabic speech. At a point in the history of Islam in Kenya, Arabic continued to enjoy great prestige as the religious language amongst globalised Muslims. In Kenya access to Arabic is limited and confined only to the highly educated graduates of Islamic universities. Kiswahili is instead used in most religious publications. The translation of the message of the Qu'ran into Kiswahili has been a major undertaking by some prominent scholars in Kenya. Kiswahili texts are available discussing an array of religious knowledge ranging from historical biographies of important personalities to contemporary issues addressing the position of women in Islam and the correctness, acceptability or error of using scientific calculations to determine the beginning of the new crescent to determine the Islamic lunar calendar.

Research challenges

The religious lives of Muslims largely revolve around the mosque, households, neighborhoods and family networks. Yet, little is known about Muslims and far less about the activities and views of its adherents. Muslim in Kenya feel that the government is increasingly interested in them in a suspicious manner and has placed them under scrutiny. As a result conducting research amongst Muslims poses unique challenges. At the outset of this research, it was feared that researching amongst the Muslim in a situation where they felt under siege was going to be problematic.

Indeed initial reluctance was noticed in almost all geographical areas covered. Muslims approached for interviews showed a tendency to suspect everybody 'carrying out' research amongst them for fear that the result will be used by the 'enemies of Islam' to undermine the Muslim community. Long hours were spent convincing Muslim leaders of the importance of having scientific data that could be useful in the community. In some cases Muslim youth expressed unfounded ideas that our research was based on or was part of some 'covert operations'.

Faced with such accusations it was important for us to exercise significant patience during the period of fieldwork to avoid confrontations. Actions like taking photographs of a mosque or a plaque indicating who sponsored the constructions of a mosque were interpreted in some areas as 'spying'. There is reluctance by Muslims to engage in self criticism. Even when Muslims have overstayed their leadership mandate in some Muslims organizations, their actions were not to be questioned. Calling on leaders of Muslims organizations for interviews meant that researchers had to be ready to be interviewed themselves on their backgrounds. Getting an adequate number of FGD participants is important for conducting efficient FGD's. During the research some FGD's failed to take place or a few respondents showed up. In such cases the research team had to mobilize other participants and set new dates and times, thereby disorganizing the time schedule of research. Some Muslim women showed enthusiasm in the FGD's although reluctance by some Muslim women meant gender representation of the result is weak.

SECTION TWO

Islam and Muslims

About 1.3 billion people worldwide consider themselves followers of Islam, the world's second largest and fast growing religion. In recent years Islam has gained influence chiefly in Africa and the central Asian countries. Islam means the complete 'submission' to God's will. A person who embraces this is a Muslim. Muslims object to being called 'Mohammedans', after the name of the Prophet Muhammad because they regard its homology to the terms 'Christian' or 'Buddhist' as misleading. Islam had its origins in the revelation that the prophet Muhammad who was born in 570 C.E. in Mecca and died in 632 A.D in Medina, is said to have received from the angel Jibril (Gabriel). People are viewed as Muslims if they publicly profess their belief that there is no God except Allah and that Muhammad is the Messenger of God. The religion of Islam is founded on the Qu'ran. Muslims believe in a life after death, a paradise, and a hell. The five 'pillars' of Islam are the belief in Allah as the only God and Muhammad as His prophet; daily prayer; giving alms; fasting during the month of Ramadan; and making pilgrimage to the holy city of Mecca at least once in a life time. In everyday life the most important pillar is the *salat*, the prayers, obligatory for all adult Muslims, which must be performed five times a day. All that is needed to hold the *salat* is a 'pure' place: a small prayer rug ensures the requisite cleanliness. Congregational prayers are held in the mosque-*masjid*, ('the place where one prostrates oneself'). The call to prayer is issued from the minaret. Typical of Islam is the close nexus of politics, religion and daily life. The Qu'ran is both a worldly and religious guide, and the *ummah* both the religious and political community.

Islam came to Kenya mainly as a companion of trade, mainly the east-west oceanic trade linking it up with the Arab countries as well as with India and the rest of the orient. Parts of Kenya however were under the sovereignty of the Sultanate of Oman whose capital was in 1840 moved from Muscat to Zanzibar, from where trade route into the interior were launched thus increasing its direct influence in Kenya. Subsequently, the rest of the country was colonized by the British albeit in steps and in two-pieces which roughly followed religious fault lines. The Kenyan interior (*bara*) mainly inhabited by adherents of indigenous African religions was first chartered to the Imperial British East African Company (1888) then transferred into a formal protectorate (1895) and subsequently 25 years later into a crown colony. The predominantly Muslim coastal strip, however, become a protectorate through an agreement with the Sultan of Zanzibar.

In Kenya Islam spread first from the coast where there is historically the largest concentration of Muslims especially in the towns of Mombasa, Malindi, Lamu and the district of Kwale. But it is difficult to fix a date for the earliest arrival and settlement of Muslims at the coast. Local traditions and chronicles of recent origin speak of Muslim settlement going back to the second caliphate, but no reliable evidence, archeological or otherwise, has been advanced to support such claims. Recently though some studies have been conducted to reveal the earliest existence of mosque ruins dating back around 800 C.E. Islam spread into the interior of Kenya only in the 19th century through trade caravans between Arabs and Swahilis and the inland tribes. Through trade, aspects of Muslims influence were implanted in the interior of Kenya. There are therefore smaller concentration of Muslims in Nairobi, Nakuru, Kisumu, Mumias, Bungoma, Kitui, Machakos, Voi, and the North Eastern Province. The main road from Mombasa to Kisumu is dotted with spaces of Islamic influences especially mosques which have been in existence since the early 20th century. However, a large number of Muslims in Kenya comprise the indigenous coastal tribes. Other upcountry communities are gradually coming under the influence of Islam.

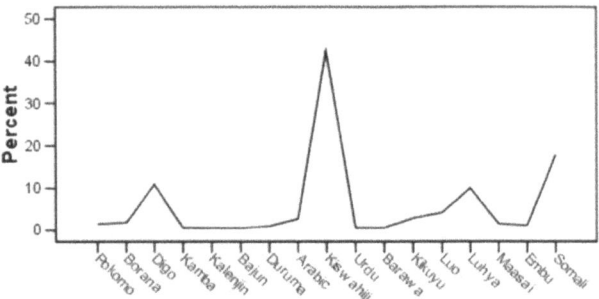

Fig. 4: Respondents first language

First language of the respondent

The effect of the spread of Islam has been the creation of a distinctive mode of life and religion, a rich historical heritage and a general ideology of universal applicability. In fact quite recently for the coastal people of East Africa, for those were the days when literate education was only an Islamic one and the only religion with claims to universality was Islam. However, the advance of colonial rule and Christianity changed this situation slowly and today, after about one thousand years of Islam in the region, Muslims in East Africa and Kenya in particular are faced with disunity and mistrust among themselves.

Main Muslim groups

The Muslim peoples of Kenya are a diverse and heterogeneous population. Muslims are found in all distinct cultural groups of the population of Kenya as identified by ethnic origin, racial division and sectarian traits. Although Muslims are diverse three peoples or communities are exceptional in their Islam. The Somali who inhabit the northern parts of the country; the Swahili communities domiciled along the coast, and the Digo living on the coast of Kenya but also extending as far as Tanzania. These three are exceptional because in comparison to the other groups of populations included in this survey they claim to have a tradition of Islam going back many centuries.

The Digo claim uniqueness as the only indigenous group, the only Bantu speaking people of Kenya to have become Muslim on a large scale. Suffice to say, the Muslim communities in Kenya today comprise various races and tribes. The main tribes are the Digo (99% muslim), Duruma (29%) and the rest of the Mijikenda tribes (20%). Others are the Pokomo (85%), Taita (6%), Swahili/Arab, Asians (60%) and Nubians (80%). Other tribes with many (but not as a majority) Muslims include the Kikuyu of Karai, Nyeri and Muranga, the Luhya of Mumias, the Akamba of Kitui and Luo in Homa Bay. North eastern tribes like the Rendille, Boran, and Galla each are about (90%) Muslim.

The presence of these three communities, the Somali, in (North Eastern Province) the Swahili (mainly in the coastal belt) and the Digo (in Kwale District), in addition to the relatively high proportion of Muslims amongst other coastal communities gives the Coast Province and North Eastern Province a marked, sometimes exclusive, Muslim character quite distinct from other parts of Kenya. Muslims communities are also found scattered in all major towns and in a number of rural villages through out the interior of Kenya.

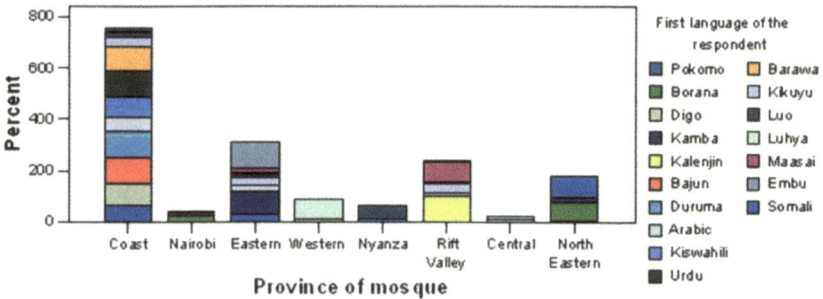

Fig. 5: Respondents language groups by province

The survey found that there is always a visible presence of Islam throughout the districts and provinces covered in the survey. However, estimating the total Muslim population of Kenya is a particularly vexing problem. It is

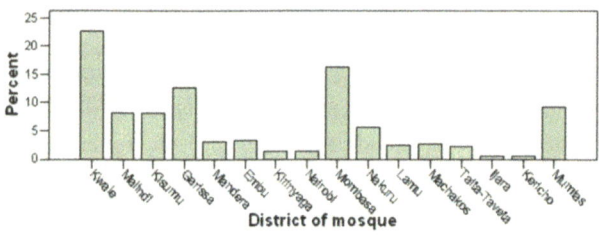

Fig. 6: Mosque distribution by district

agreed that Muslims constitute a minority group but the proportion of this minority remains contentious. Non-Muslim sources estimate Muslims to be between six to eleven percent (6-11%) of the total population of Kenya estimated to be about 32 million.

Projections from Muslim sources tend to put Muslim population between fifteen to twenty five percent (15-25%) of the total population of Kenya. Difficulties in estimating how many Kenyans are Muslims become further compounded because the 1999 census gave some hope of resolving the issue since religious affiliation was included as a question. However, no analysis of responses to that question was published. Such a statistic is not likely to appear soon given the sensitivity of the matter to both government and communities concerned.

Being a minority religious group Muslims tend to be the most disadvantaged. It has been claimed that social, economic, educational and political developments have been slow in coming to Muslim populated areas. Muslim capacity to compete with other communities in most respects is rather limited. As a result Muslims continue to complain about lack of concerted effort on the part of government and community leadership to adequately address the dire needs of Muslims as they face the basic problems of life, including poor or no education, unemployment, exposure to harmful disease, lack of adequate health facilities and serious social hazards.

Muslim ideological communities

The Muslim communities in Kenya today consist of all the major ideological groups in Islam. The Sunni are the most dominant and majority group which consists mainly of African Muslims. There are also Sunni amongst Muslims of Arab and South East Asian origins.

The majority of Muslims in Kenya follow

mostly Shafii *madhhab* and persuasions. Shiite Muslims are mostly of the Ithna-ashari and Bohra groups. Shiite Muslims, mostly of Asian origins may appear insignificant numerically, but socially and economically they have made their mark. Together with the Hindus they control much of the trading and industrial activities of East Africa.

They have played a vital and indispensable role in the economic and social development of this region. Moreover, the Asian Muslims of East Africa form the largest non-African Muslim group in tropical

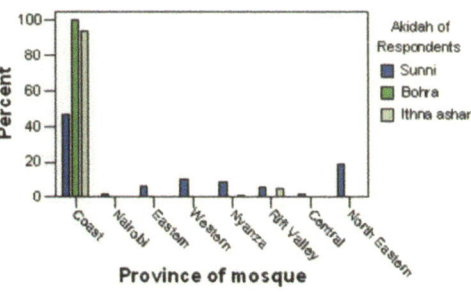

Fig. 8: Distribution of Muslim akidah by province

Fig. 7: Muslim groups by akidah

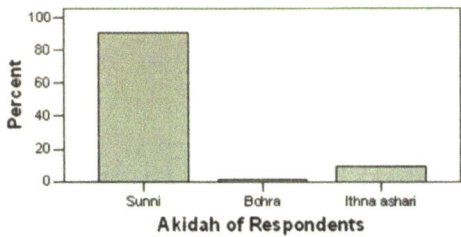

Africa. Shafii Muslims are more united but Shiites have other divisions. One of these, the Nazari Muslims or (Khojas) is the best organized Muslim community in Kenya today. Their religious, social and fiscal affairs are highly centralized under their spiritual leader, the Aga Khan. The other group is the Mustalian Ismailia (or Bohras) who are not much different from the former. The last group are the Ithna-asharis (or Twelvers), a part of the Shiite sect they originated in Persia and India.

The Coast Province has the most diverse sectarian distribution of Muslims. The largest concentration of Shiites especially the Bohra and the Ithna-ashari community is mostly found in the Coast Province. Shiite Muslims are also concentrated in the districts of Rift Valley Province especially Nakuru which has a significant population of Ithna-ashari Muslims.

Muslim religious practices

Muslims universally hold two major celebrations - each of which last three days. The Feast of the Sacrifice (*Eid al Adha*) reminds Muslims that Allah commanded Ibrahim (Abraham) to sacrifice Ismail, one of his own sons. After Allah saw that Ibrahim was faithful and could obey Him, he ended the trial and allowed him to sacrifice a lamb instead. During *Eid al Adha*, this starts on the 10th day of the month in which Muslims make the pilgrimage to Mecca, (*Dhul-Hijja*). Families slaughter a sheep, a cow, camel or goat whichever they can afford. A portion of the sacrifice must be given as charity to the poor. The other festival is *Eid al Fitr* celebrated after the end of Ramadan fasting; a time of dawn to dusk abstinence.

How Muslims in Kenya practice faith is differentiated by specific activities meant to display religious consciousness and spirituality. These included *dhikr*, attendance at *mawlid*, involvement in propagation activities like the *da'awa* and *mihadhara* and participating in the endeavor to acquire Islamic knowledge and awakening through a habitual attendance at mosque lectures (*darsa*).

Fig. 9: Dhikr items

Dhikr is an ancient spiritual practice where Muslims attempted to enter into a state of closeness to God through a continuous recitation of Allah's names and His attributes. This practice was popular in the early 1960-1970s as the spiritual practice amongst most Muslims who are influenced by Sufi inclinations.

In the early 1980s Sufi inclinations began to decline as a strong purist interpretation of Islam began to gather ground in Kenya. However, old habits die hard and Muslims continue to organize and attend *dhikr* session in order to seek closeness to Allah. The survey found out that the majority of Muslims either 'always' attended *dhikr* or 'occasionally' found time to attend. About forty five percent (45%) of Muslims who participated in the survey said they would 'never attend' *dhikr* rituals. Muslims who 'always' attend *dhikr* range from thirty to thirty two percent (30-32%), while up to twenty percent (20%) of Muslims 'occasionally' attend *dhikr* sessions.

Like the *dhikr*, the *mawlid* too is a common feature in the Muslim ritual calendar. Sometimes *mawlid* has generated controversy amongst Muslims. There are Muslims who support its performance and others are ardently opposed to celebrating the birth of the prophet. Those opposed have branded the *mawlid* a *bid'a* (innovation).

Generally, Muslims attended *mawlid* but the percentage of those who were opposed is

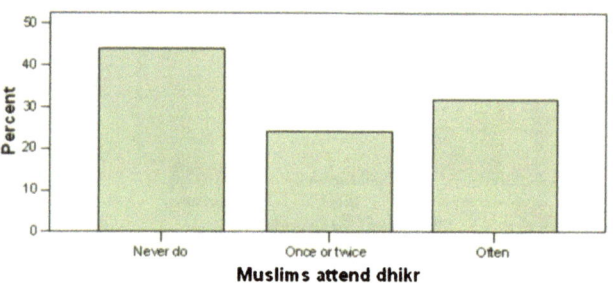

Fig. 10: Muslim attendance to dhikr

equally significant. About forty eight percent (48%) of Muslims often attended *mawlid* whenever they were held, between five to seven percent (5-7%) had been to the *mawlid* perhaps once or twice by the time the survey was undertaken. However, forty three percent (43%) of Muslims polled said they would never attend a *mawlid*. The chart below shows the distribution of attendance to *dhikr* by the province of the mosques.

Figure 12 shows the distribution of Muslims who attended *mawlid* in the provinces as follows;

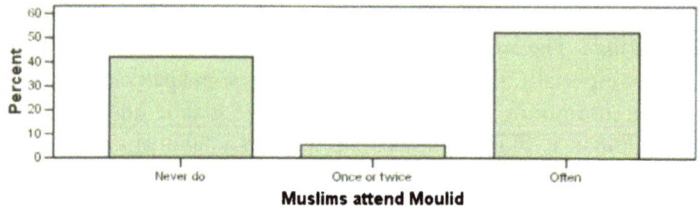

Fig. 11: Muslim attendance to mawlid

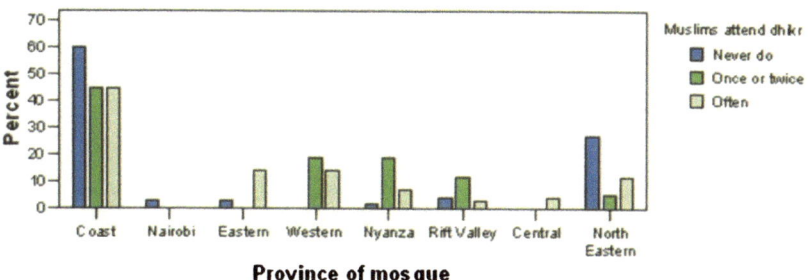

Fig. 12: Muslim attendance to dhikr by province

Muslims who attend *mawlid* were in the majority in Coast Province, the percentage of those who never attended *mawlid* was the same as those who attended once or twice. In North Eastern Province the majority of Muslims will never attend a *mawlid* celebration, a slightly lower figure occasionally attended *mawlid* while a very small percentage had a habit to attend *mawlid* as often as they were held. Most Muslims would attend the *mawlid* in Western Province compared with those who will not.

The percentage of those for whom the *mawlid* is popular or not popular in the province may indicate the influence of purist practice in Islam associated with Wahhabi tendencies. In provinces where *mawlid* is popular Wahhabi teachings appear not to be strong but in those provinces where *mawlid* appears a religious aberration the most likely explanation would be that Wahhabi anti-*mawlid* tendencies have gained ground.

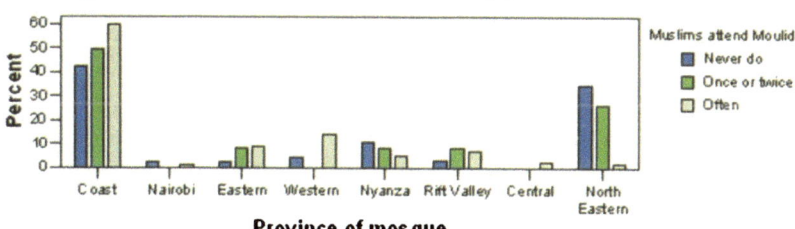

Fig. 13: Muslim attendance to mawlid by province

Most mosques are actively involved in outreach activities especially *da'awa* (attempts to spread the message of Islam). The most active *da'awa* groups in Kenya including the *tabligh* and *markaz da'awa* groups. The Bilal Muslims Mission is a strong Shiite propagation group. These *da'awa* groups usually establish networks of preachers who visit rural Mosques teaching communities about Islam. In some places *da'awa* groups criticize local tradition and Islamic observances leading to ideological conflicts and denunciation. In Kwale District, South Asian (*tabligh*) *da'awa* groups were generally resented and named '*watu wa kulala miskitini*' (those/people who sleep in the mosque), but local groups who hold annual vigils (*markaz*) during the last week of December every year are popular with Muslims on the coast.

In the chart next page (Fig. 14), the survey found that about seventy percent (70%) of

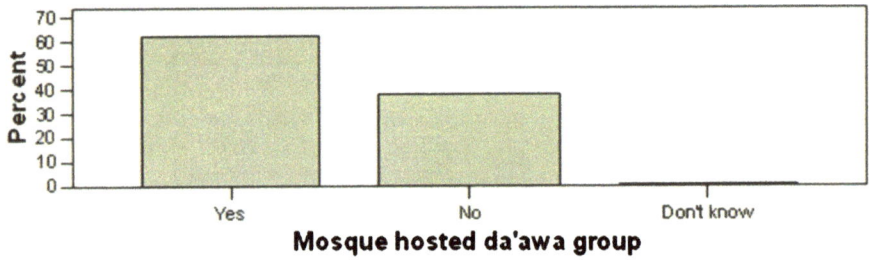

Fig. 14: Percentages of mosques hosting da'awa groups

mosques had hosted a *da'awa* group although a significant percentage appears not to have been visited by any such groups. The chart below shows the extent at which mosques have hosted *da'awa* groups in the provinces during year 2005.

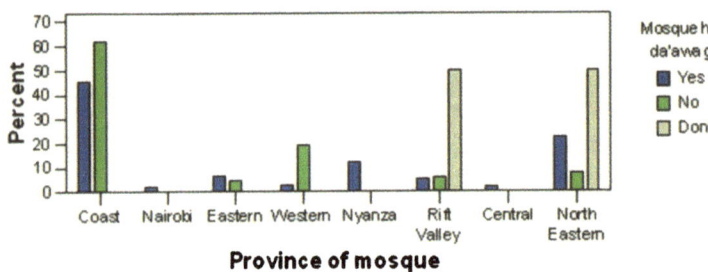

Fig. 15: Percentages of mosques hosting da'awa groups by province

Generally, the majority of mosques indicated that they had hosted a *da'awa* group. All mosques in Nairobi and Central Province included in this survey had hosted an outreach group. In the rest of the provinces a majority of mosques responded "yes" to having hosted a *da'awa* group.

Mihadhara

Public meetings to discuss and hear about different religious topics are a common feature in Kenya. Amongst Muslims such gathering, (*mihadhara*) are usually held in neighborhoods or other public places. During the *mihadhara*, itinerant Muslim preachers mount huge public address systems and engage fellow Muslims or followers of other religion in a 'debate', 'discussion' 'dialogue' or 'competition' on religious topics. *Mihadhara* gatherings can be huge and sometimes controversial especially those with an inclination to engage in a discussion of comparative religion.

The chart below (Fig. 17) shows that *mihadhara* are generally popular with Muslims in Kenya. About sixty six percent (66%) of

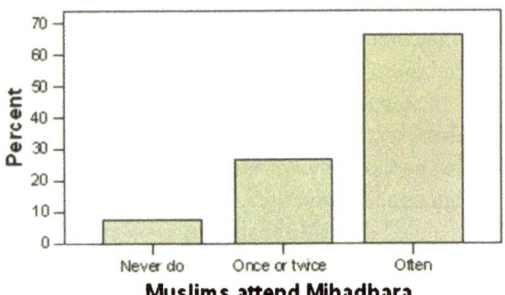

Fig. 16: Muslim attendance to mihadhara

Muslims indicated that it was a habit for them to 'always' attend *mihadhara*. Those who occasionally found time to attend *mihadhara* comprised twenty eight percent (28%) while a small percentage of the survey six percent (6%), 'never' attend public religious meetings. The chart below shows the extent at which Muslims in different provinces attend *mihadhara*.

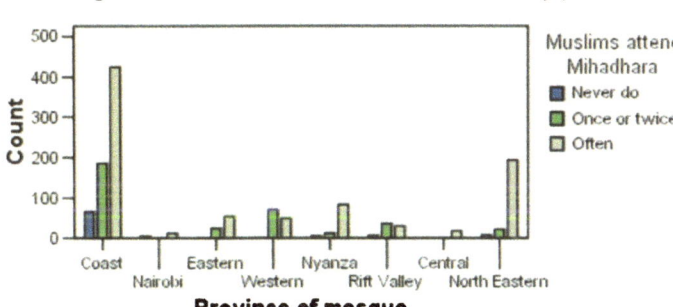

Fig. 17: Muslim attendance to mihadhara by province

Surprisingly *mihadhara* did not appear to be popular amongst Muslims polled in the Coast Province. About sixty eight percent (68%) of respondents in the survey who did not attend *mihadhara* were from Coast Province. The majority of Muslims in North Eastern Province are those who will always attend *mihadhara*. In Nairobi most Muslims will never attend *mihadhara* while in Western Province a majority of Muslims are those who occasionally found the time to attend public preaching sessions.

Darsa

Another occasion where Muslims have the opportunity to attend public discussions on religion is the *darsa* or mosque lectures. *Darsa* are gatherings held in the mosque where the local *alim* or an invited scholar will discuss a special topic. Whenever they are held *darsa* tend to be formal and structured. Those in attendance at a *darsa* session are expected to listen as they wait for their opportunity to ask questions at the end of the lecture. Not every Muslim scholar has the opportunity to give a *darsa* in some of the largest mosques. To be invited to give a *darsa* in a particular mosque signifies respect. For a popular *alim* to be giving *darsa* in certain mosques also symbolizes the importance of the mosque and its position in society.

The chart below (Fig. 18) shows that *darsa* are equally popular amongst all Muslims. About eighty two percent (82%) of respondents in the survey said they 'always' at-

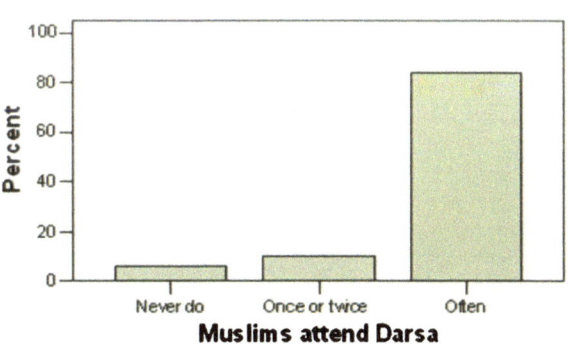

Fig. 18: Muslim attendance to darsa

tend *darsa*, while eleven percent (11%) attended occasionally. A few Muslims polled in this survey did not attend *darsa*. The chart below shows the distribution of Muslims who attend *darsa*. Note that no Muslims in Nairobi, Eastern, Western, Nyanza and Central Provinces missed the opportunity to attend *darsa* while Muslim in Coast, Rift Valley and North Eastern Province often did afford not to attend *darsa*.

The majority of Muslims who did not attend *darsa* were polled from North Eastern Province. Nairobi provided a small percentage of Muslims polled in this survey but all indicated that they would always attend *darsa*. All Muslims in Eastern, Nyanza and Central Provinces attend *darsa* although figures varied; some will always attend and some who will occasionally attend.

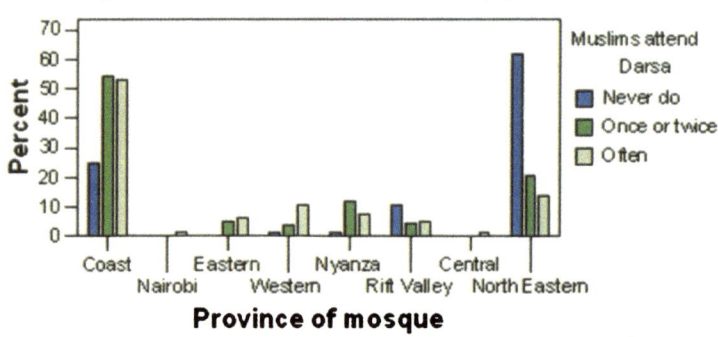

Fig. 19: Muslim attendance to darsa by province

SECTION THREE

Mosque construction

A mosque (or *masjid*) is defined as an Islamic institution that conducts amongst others but significantly the Friday prayers (the *jumaah*) and organizes other religious activities to serve a population of Muslims. The mosques of Kenya are old and new, modern and ruins. The building of mosques has fluctuated since early 19th century. A few mosques are older having decade of early 1980s to the 1990s. Mosques built during this period constitute twenty five percent (25%) of the survey data. The decade of the 1990's shows significant expansion of the number of mosques in Kenya perhaps signifying a concerted effort by Muslims to expand not only in the regions where Islam was already an established way of life but also into new areas. Building of mosques has continued apace then. The survey recorded a further expansion;

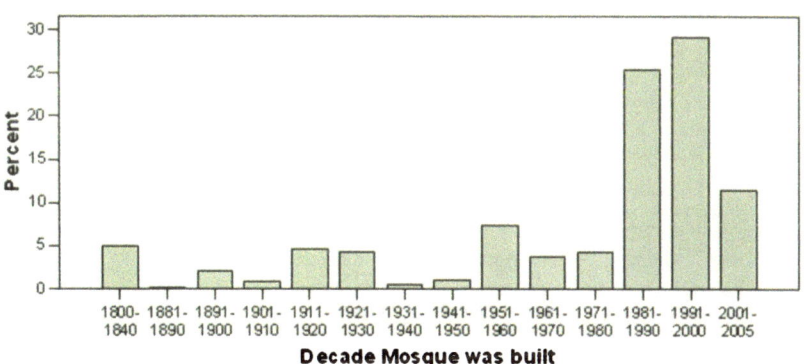

Fig. 20: Mosque construction by decade

been built during the decades from 1800-1840. Although the survey identified mosques from that period, historical sources and archeological discoveries point to earlier contacts between Muslims from the Arabian Peninsula and the communities of the coast of eastern Africa dating back to the 9th century. The chart above shows the expansion and decline of the construction of mosques over the century.

However, from the decade up to 1840, the building of mosques appears sporadic. But there was an expansion of mosques in the decades of the 1950s to 1960s followed by a slight decline during the 1970s through to late 1980s. The building of mosques increased from the close to thirty eight percent (38%) of the mosques were built during the decade after the 1990s. Since 2001 a decline in the building of mosques has been predicted as imminent due to restrictions placed on the transfer of funds as a result of measures to curtail terrorism.

The survey shows that Muslims are found in almost every district and province of Kenya. Thus mosques included in this survey are located in cities, rural villages, urban areas and towns. About eighty seven percent (87%) of mosques include in this survey are located in rural and urban areas. Village mosques account for less than ten percent (10%); mosques located in the major cities comprised less than five percent (5%) of data included in this survey. This distribution can imply that Islam in Kenya remains an urban religion although there are some attempts to conduct *da'awa* to spread Islam in rural areas of Kenya.

Distribution of mosques in the provinces

The survey collected data from mosques in eight administrative provinces of Kenya including Coast, Nairobi, Central, Eastern, Western, Nyanza, Rift Valley, and North Eastern Provinces. Forty four percent (44%) of mosques selected are in the Coast Province; North Eastern Province provided nineteen percent (19%); Western Kenya contributed eleven percent (11%); while Nyanza comprised data from slightly lower than ten percent (10%).

The percentages both in terms of respondents and mosques covered in this survey corresponds to the demographic composition and sparse distribution of Muslims in Kenya. But, these results cannot be used to make claims to the exact account of a Muslim demography in Kenya. The survey methods fall far too short for such a claim. However, the results can be used to estimate the distribution of Muslims in the administrative provinces of Kenya. The findings of this survey confirm that most Muslims reside predominately in the Coast Province. A mosque count in the Coast Province shows that Kwale District has the highest number of mosques.

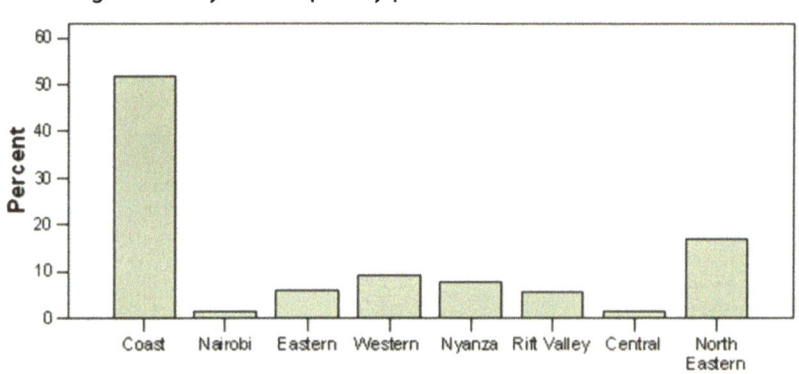

Fig. 21: Surveyed mosques by province

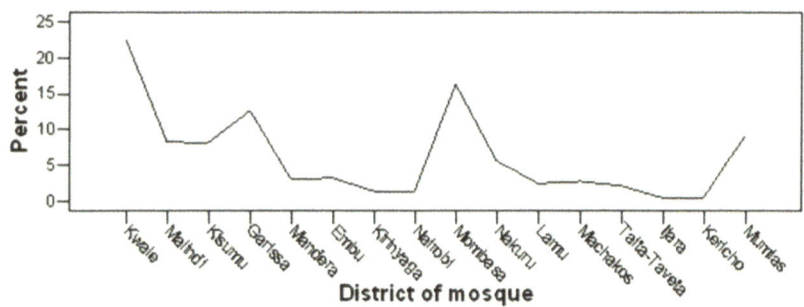

Fig. 22: Surveyed mosques by district

Distribution of mosques in the districts

The sixteen districts covered in the survey included Kwale, Malindi, Kisumu, Garissa, Embu, Kirinyaga, Nairobi, Mombasa, Nakuru, Lamu, Machakos, Taita-Taveta, Ijara, Kericho, Mandera, and Mumias. Kwale District in Coast Province accounts for twenty eight percent (28%) of the data.[1] Garissa District accounts for eighteen percent (18%). Other districts, Kisumu, Nakuru and the town of Mumias contributed a significant though lower ratio of the mosques included in the survey this might mean that Muslims populations in these districts are much lower.

Registration of mosques

The establishment of mosques in Kenya appears to conform to government procedures especially in relation to registrations. Most mosques indicated they are registered under a government law. Seventy and seventy five percent (70-75%) of mosques included in the survey responded 'yes' to the question 'Is mosque registered with Government?' Mosques preferred to register under a variety of legal statutes including Wakf Law, Societies Act, Association and Trust Deed. Some

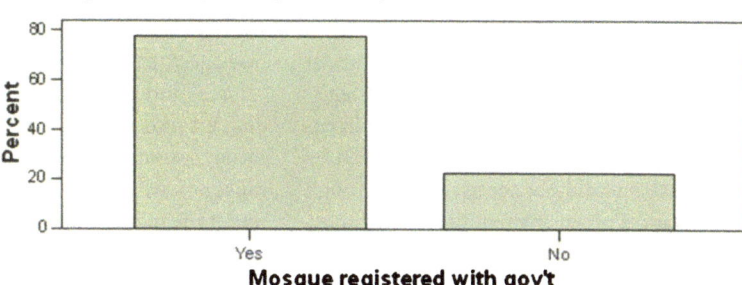

Fig. 23: Mosques registered by law

mosques appeared registered with government departments.

Mosques registered as Muslim pious endowments (*wakf* or *awqaf*) comprised about forty three percent (43%) of all mosques. Mosques registered under the Societies Act comprise twenty nine percent (29%); less than five percent (5%) of mosques are registered under government departments including mosques in institutions like the Prisons and the Armed Forces. Between ten to fifteen percent (10%-

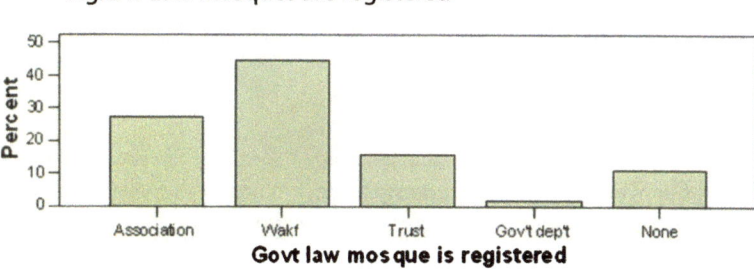

Fig. 24: Law mosques are registered

---

1) *Independent data collected by the CIPK shows that Kwale District has the largest percentage of mosques in the expansive and Muslim dominated Coast Province.*

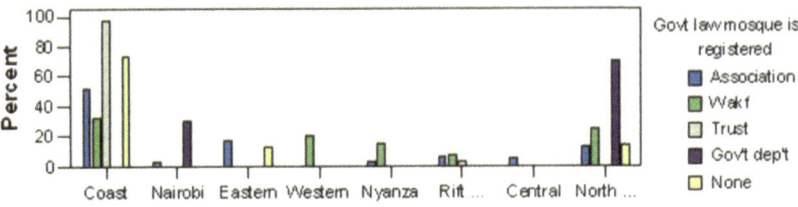

Fig. 25: Mosques registered by province

15%) of mosques were not registered under any of the available laws, perhaps not registered at all. Such mosques were mostly in rural areas where they stand on land owned by individuals and did not necessarily go through a registration process when built. Most mosques in urban areas will be required to adhere to proper building plans and have them approved and registered with the local authorities. Such procedures mean that a mosque will have to identify with a certain statute of registration. Preferences for registering mosques varied from province to province.

The Coast Province has the highest percentage of registered mosques comprising between sixty five to sixty nine percent (65%-69%) of those polled. Western Province and Rift Valley has all its mosques polled in this survey registered with the government. Mosques in the Coast Province are registered in all statutes available, except that no mosque appeared registered as a government department. Mosques registered as government departments are found in Nairobi and North Eastern Province. Central Province had mosques only registered under Societies Act, through Muslim associations, while Western Province appears to favor the registration of mosques as *wakf*.

Mosque sponsorship, leadership and organization

Various categories, local and foreign, of sponsors undertake the building, maintenance, and management of mosques.

Local and foreign sponsors can be further divided into individual, corporate or organizational sponsors. The survey found that most mosques were constructed, sponsored and under the management of local communities, including local groups and organizations. Local sponsors of mosques comprise about fifty two percent (52%) of all sponsors of mosques in Kenya. Local individual Muslims constitute about thirty percent (30%) of all spon-

Fig. 26: Plaque of Sponsor-Tanzila Jamia Mosque

sors. The rest foreign sponsors of mosques include both foreign individuals and organizations.

Close to twenty percent (20%) of mosques in Kenya were constructed by and continue to be managed by foreign sponsors. Examples of major foreign based sponsors include Rabita (World Muslims League), and Africa Muslim Agency and the International Islamic

Fig. 27: Plaque of mosques sponsored by foreign organization

Relief Organization (IIRO). Since 1998 Muslims have raised concern that the state has been placing obstacles that have hampered the building of mosques and sponsorship by foreign organization. In its attempts to curb the transfer of funds to suspected 'terrorist' organizations the state outlawed some Muslim charities for example the Ibrahim al Ibrahim Foundation leading to an accusation of harassment from the Muslim community.

During the survey mosques leaders and participants were asked to indicate the style of management used to run their affairs by responding to the question 'is there a constitution at the mosque which guides and gives rule for effective management?' Sixty eight percent (68%) of mosques do not use a constitution to assist in the management of their affairs. This seeming anomaly was more notable in some provinces than others. About fifty seven percent (57%) of mosques without a constitution were found in the Coast Province. In North Eastern Province, ten percent (10%) of its mosques are without a constitution. Mosques in Eastern Province had the highest ratio with a constitution.

Given the majority of mosques do not have a constitution as a guideline for managing affairs, how then are they run? To manage the day to day affairs of mosques worshippers may choose to establish a management commit-

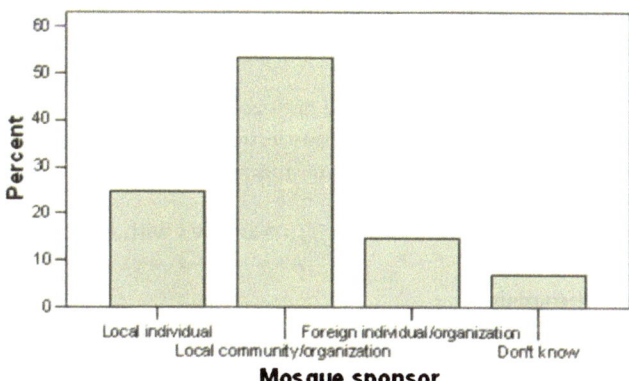

Fig. 28: Mosque sponsors by category

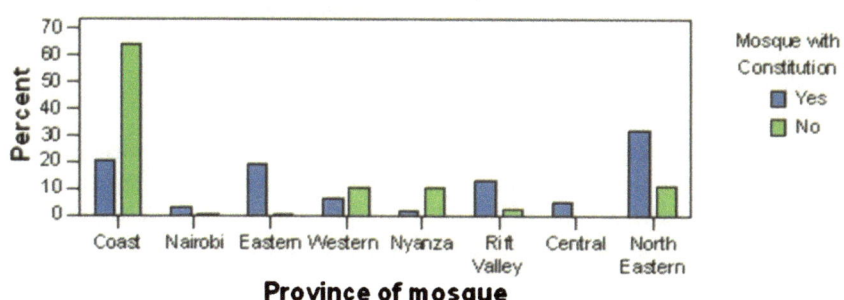

Fig. 29: Mosque with constitution in province

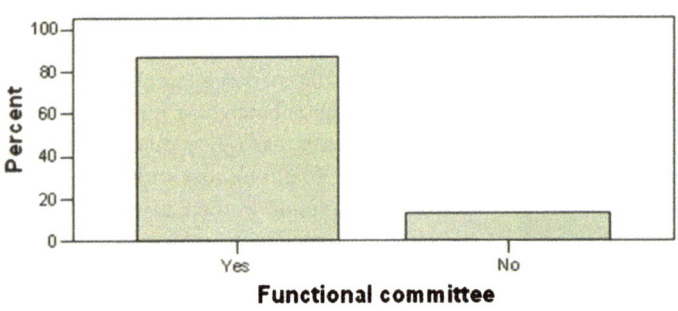

Fig. 30: Mosque with functional committee

The chart illustrates that Muslims do not particularly favor elections as a method to establish mosque committees. In response to the question whether the mosque committee was elected or not, fifty three percent (53%) of worshippers responded 'no', that is there are no elections held for the mosque committee. This did not in anyway indicate that respondents were in favor of elections, simply elections were not held at the mosque in which they were *ratibs*. Respondents also complained that lack of elections for the committee in mosques always leads to suspicion amongst Muslims in mosques that were well endowed financially.

tee. Most mosques have a management committee but these were considered not to function up to expectations. Even when mosques established management committee they did not necessarily have a constitution or a legal framework in which the mosque was managed.

This means that mosques did not necessarily hold any document or a constitution as significant in the management of mosque affairs but nevertheless recognized the need to establish a committee that would function to manage affairs of the mosque. Members of mosque committees are volunteers either nominated by mosque sponsors or benefactors. In cases where mosque construction is associated with individual local benefactors such sponsors usually assumed the ownership of the mosque as a property.

The chart above (fig. 30) shows that an overwhelming majority, eighty percent (80%) of mosques in Kenya are managed by an existing and functioning committee.

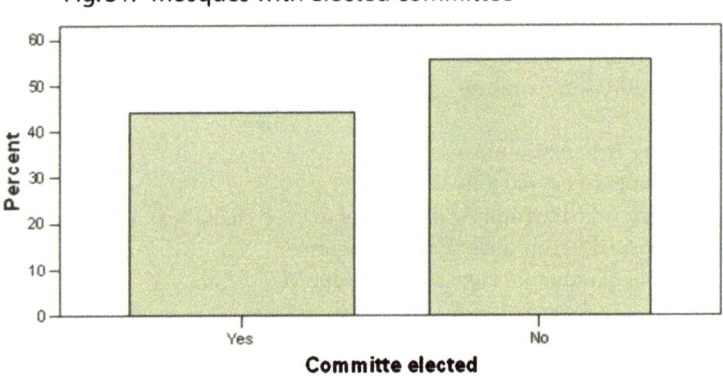

Fig. 31: Mosques with elected committee

Mosque finances

The question of mosque finances is one of those that lead to suspicion when researchers put it directly to Muslims. Mosque officials will barely reveal how much money or property belongs to the mosques. Thus, how well or not well endowed mosques were is a common complaint amongst Muslims in Kenya. The tendency for Muslims to accuse mosque officials of misappropriation of mosque resources has on many occasions led to conflicts that ended up in courts of law for arbitration. Perhaps transparency about the financial position of the mosque can be used to minimize perennial conflict and accusations of misappropriation of resources. During the survey a tabulation of figures was initially given to Muslims to allow them to indicate their assessment of the financial position of mosques. When this proved 'difficult', they were asked to make general statements about the financial position of their mosques. The chart above (Fig. 32) tabulated the responses.

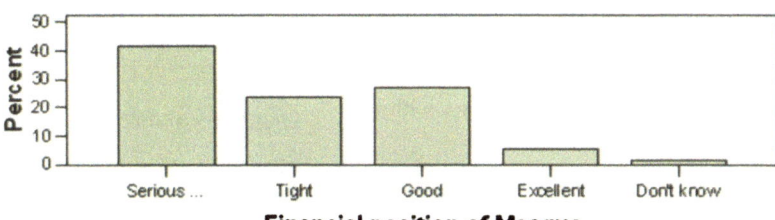

Fig. 32: Financial position of mosque

nancial position. A small proportion about five percent (5%) of the mosques in the survey boast of an excellent financial status. There were Muslims who did not know of the financial positions of the mosques in which they considered themselves members. Muslims accounted for the poor financial position of mosques by referring to two main factors. First, was lack of enthusiasm by the majority

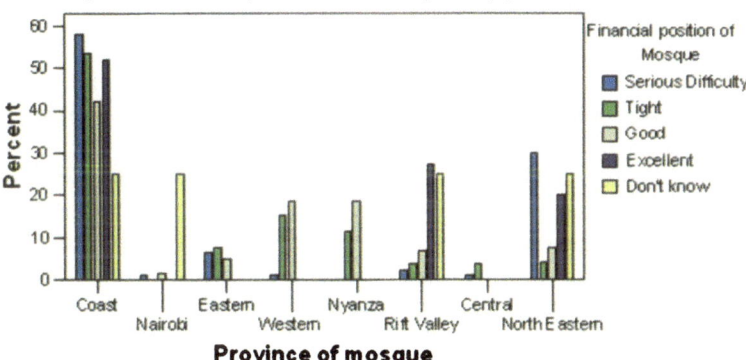

Fig. 33: Financial position of mosques by province

Between the ranges of 'excellent', 'good' and 'difficulty', the majority of mosques considered their financial standing to be in 'serious difficulty'. About sixty five percent (65%) of mosques did not consider their financial position to be healthy; they faced serious financial difficulties. About twenty percent (20%) of Mosques in this survey were in a good financial position.

of Muslims to make direct financial commitment towards the upkeep of the mosque. The majority of respondents thought that local Muslims should be encouraged to participate actively in mosque programs including taking care of the financial health of the mosque. The second factor that contributed to the poor financial position of mosques was that since the terrorist attack in Kenya, the government has been monitoring the movement of foreign funds from Muslims into Kenya. Because Muslims, were largely dependent on funds from foreign donors to manage mosque affairs such measures have hindered the improvement of the financial situation of most mosques.

The majority of mosques whose financial status was said to be in serious difficulties are found in the Coast Province.

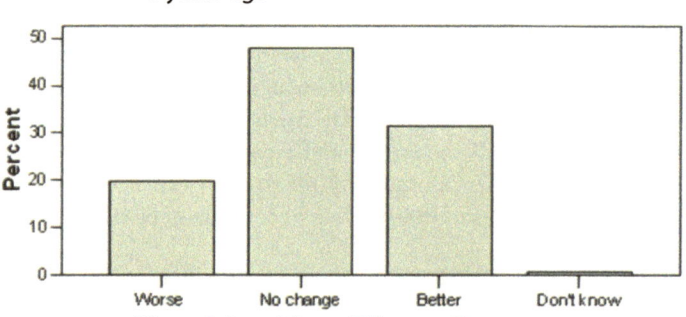

Fig. 34: Financial position of mosque compared to 5 years ago

Since the year 2000 when measures to hinder the transfer of funds to Muslim organizations were put in place, the financial condition of most mosques has moved negatively over the past five years. About twenty percent (20%) of mosques have developed a worse financial status since the year 2000. About thirty eight percent (38%) of mosques have remained in almost the same (poor) financial position since the last five years while thirty two percent (32%) indicated that their financial position has improved and it was better compared to the last five years.

Disputes at the mosques

Being social institutions mosques have from time to time faced institutional difficulties. Communities that use mosques sometimes disagree subsequently leading to disputes. Some of the most common reported disputes in the mosque involve replacement of mosque leadership including Imams and other officials, financial (*mis*) management, questions of *fiqh* and *akidah* and interfaith disputes. This survey sought Muslim opinion on such occurrences at the mosques.

Generally, mosques in Kenya experience few disputes over the replacement of Imams. About seventy percent (70%) of the mosques reported did not have or experienced disputes on the replacement of their Imam. Around

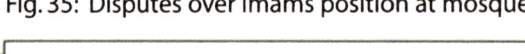

Fig. 35: Disputes over Imams position at mosque

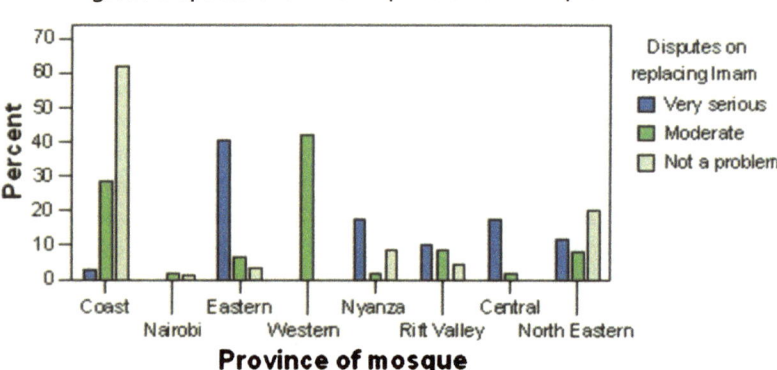

twenty percent (20%) thought that disputes did occur but they were moderate, while less than five percent (5%) reported as having experienced 'very serious disputes' involving attempts to replace the Imam.

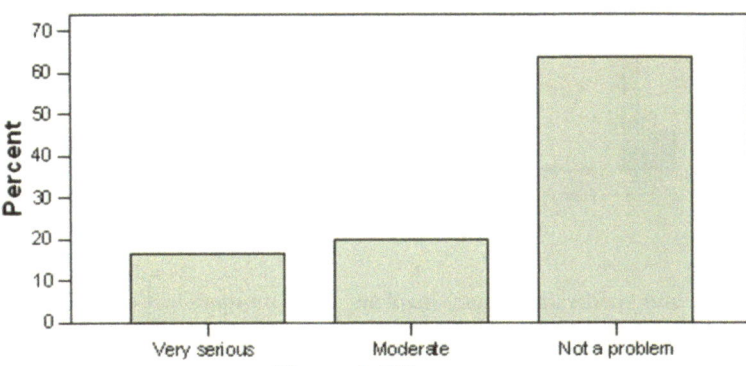

Fig. 36: Disputes over financial (mis)management at mosque

The majority of mosques on the Coast, North Eastern, and Nyanza did not experience disputes involving the replacement of the Imam. Most mosques in Central Province experienced 'serious' and 'moderate' difficulties involving the replacement of the Imam. The majority of mosques in Western Province experienced difficulties with replacing Imams but such disputes were reported to be 'moderate.' When disputes centered on the replacement of Imams occur they are as a result of conflict over religious practice or ideology (*akidah*). For example, mosque followers could have a long tradition of holding the *mawlid* and the imams will be expected to conform to this tradition. If he does not then some worshippers might attempt to have him replaced with another who will be more favorable to the practice. The reverse may also be the case when the Imam declines to uphold a long tradition of religious practice at certain mosques.

Apart from conflict based on religious practice, the management of mosque finances was reported to have caused serious difficulties in about fifteen percent (15%) of the mosques in the survey, while close to twenty percent (20%) of mosques experienced moderate difficulties with how mosque finances were managed.

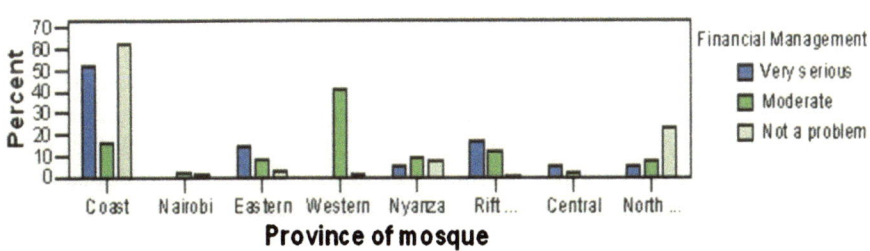

Fig. 37: Disputes over mosque finance by province

Mosques in Central Province reported the highest concentration of 'very serious' difficulties involving financial mismanagement of mosques. Nyanza Province had the least responses indicating 'serious difficulties'. Majority of mosque in Rift Valley recorded 'very

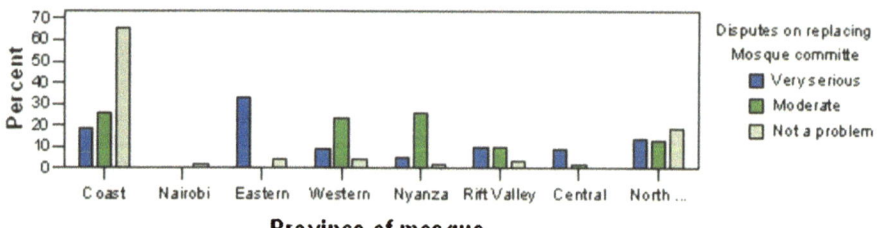

Fig. 38: Disputes over replacing mosque committee by province

serious' and 'moderate' disputes involving financial mismanagement.

Mosque committees in Kenya appear fairly stable once in office. Sixty two percent (62%) of mosques reported not to have experienced problems with their management committee. Twenty percent (20%) thought there were 'moderate' disputes involving the way mosque committees were replaced. Central and Eastern Provinces experienced the most 'serious' difficulties with replacement of mosque committees: the majority of mosques in Nairobi did not experiences any problems while the majority of mosques in Nyanza reported 'moderate' problems.

Matters having to do with religious practice; interpretation of lawful and unlawful, being normative and legalistic questions, appears as the most disputed in the mosques in Kenya. About seventy percent (70%) of mosques had experienced disputes involving matters of *fiqh* (legalistic interpretations-jurisprudence) and *akidah*. A few mosques, five percent (5%) reported there were no such disputes in the mosques, while twenty percent (20%) indicated having recognized disputes on *akidah* and *fiqh* but characterized their occurrence as 'moderate'.

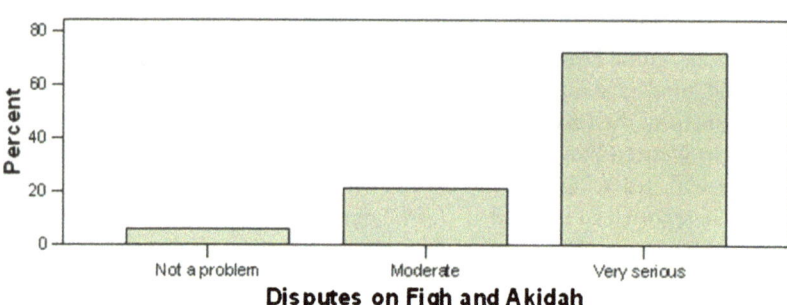

Fig. 39: Mosques experience disputes on fiqh and akidah

Almost all provinces reported to have experienced 'very serious' disputes on *fiqh* and *akidah* with an exception of mosques in Nyanza Province where the majority of disputes were thought to be 'moderate.' In Central Province most mosques did not experience disputes concerning these matters.

Most common interfaith disputes that might occur and involve mosque have to do with minor misunderstandings between communities of different faith traditions especially between Muslims and Christians. Some of these disputes include complaints over perceived disturbances cause to non Muslims by the early morning *adhan*. Sometimes non

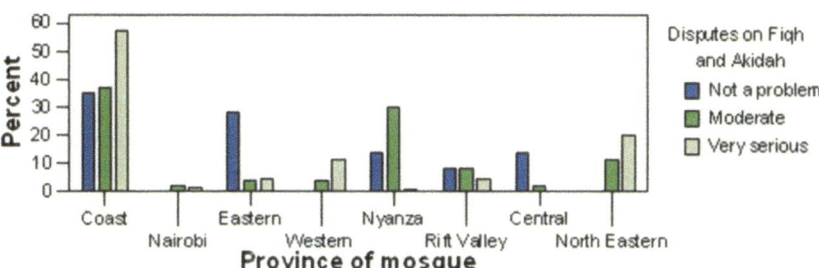

Fig. 40: Disputes over fiqh and akidah by province

Muslims have complained over the construction of mosques in emerging middle class neighborhoods citing over population and possible devaluing of property but these are minimal and usually resolved amicable. There are cases where non-Muslims have attempted to offend Muslims by committing action deemed desecrating Muslims places of worship. However, the majority of mosques in Muslim dominated areas did not experience inter-faith disputes.

Western Province had the highest ratio of mosques which did not experience interfaith disputes. In Nairobi a third of the mosques experienced serious interfaith disputes, a third recorded moderate disputes and the rest third did not experience inter-faith related disputes.

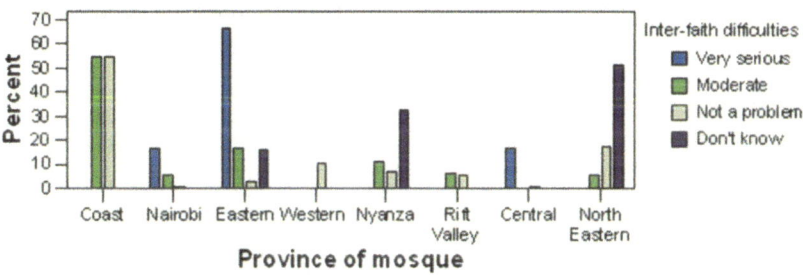

Fig. 41: Inter-faith disputes at mosque by province

SECTION FOUR

Imams

Imams are the leaders of *salat* in the mosque. They perform the most significant role in leading worship during the five obligatory *salat* times. Most mosques have regular Imams, that is, an individual whom the community and *ratibs* of the mosque expected to avail themselves to lead others during *salat*. Eighty six percent (86%) of mosques said the Imam at the mosque was in regular employment there. This shows continuity of spiritual leadership at the mosques. The presence of regular Imams also show some sense of good organization for guiding spiritual matters. Because of the significant role, both spiritual and temporal that Imams perform in the Muslim community, the survey was interested in a number of issues concerning the Imam's work at the mosque. The survey was particularly keen to ask about the nature of the Imams' vocation, where Imams acquired their skills and knowledge, levels of learning attained, the use of sacred texts, forms, and sources of articulation of Islamic knowledge by the Imam, and the existence of networks.

As indicated, mosques have regular Imams who are also salaried employees at the mosques. Fifty five percent (55%) of Imams receive a salary from one source of mosque finances or another. However, a significant percentage is regular at the mosque but do not receive any remuneration. These perform their roles in a voluntary capacity. In mosques where the Imam receives remuneration, funding is usually sourced locally from local community, local organizations and local individuals. Local communities contribute about fifty percent (50%) of the funds going towards the Imam's upkeep. Other contributions, though insignificant are sourced from foreign individuals. Both local and foreign individuals contribute but not in any significant way to the remuneration of Imams in Kenya. It is not possible to give details of individuals and organizations that support the remuneration of Imams at the mosque. Muslims consider this a guarded secret on two points. First is

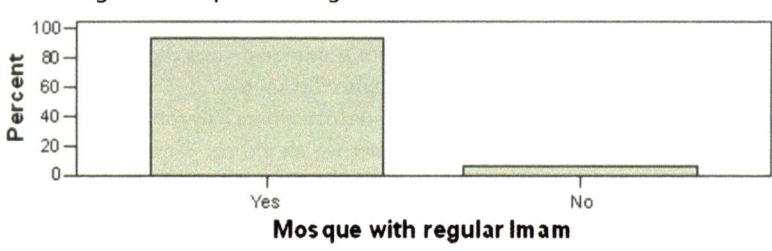

Fig. 42: Mosque with regular Imam

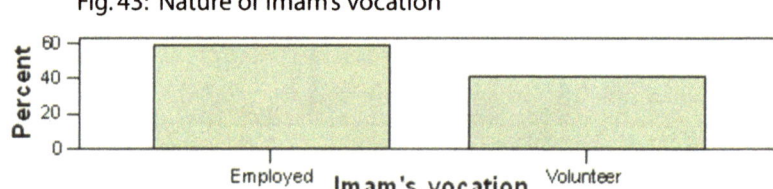

Fig. 43: Nature of Imam's vocation

Fig. 44: Imam's position advertised at Jamia Mosque-Nairobi

POSITION OF IMAM cum KHATEEB

The MAJLIS OF JAMIA MASJID COMMITTEE invites applications for the position of IMAM cum KHATEEB

The applicant should be a Sunni Muslim possessing the following minimum qualifications: -

- A Bachelors degree from a recognised Islamic university in Islamic studies
- At least five years experience in a similar position and /or Da'wah related activities
- Preferably a *Hafidh ul Quran* with excellent *qira'ah*
- Fluent in both written and spoken Arabic, Kiswahili and English. Any other language would be an added advantage.
- A Kenya citizen, with a minimum of 35 years of age
- Excellent public speaking skills with good public relations
- Dynamic, dedicated and highly motivated

An attractive salary package with ultra modern apartment would be provided to the successful candidate
Please apply with detailed testimonials (photocopies) with at least three reputable (3) referees who are well known in the Islamic field.
NOTE: All applicants who had applied for the above position in response to the advertisements appearing in the daily newspaper on 25th July 2005 need not re-apply

tractive remuneration. Generally, Imams are lowly paid unless they work for the most organized mosque communities like the Jamia Mosques in Nairobi. It is interesting to note that organizations like the Jamia mosque make specific requirements setting some precedents on how in the future Imams may be appointed. In the case of Jamia mosque the job description asked for the following qualifications: bachelors degree from an Islamic University, long experiences in a similar position, perfection in melodious and correct (*qira'ah*) recitation of the Qur'an, competent (*hafidh*) memorizer, fluency in Arabic, Kiswahili and English, Dynamic, dedicated and highly motivated.

the religious based explanation that individuals who sponsor Imams' salaries are doing it *fi-sabilillah* (for the sake of Allah); hence they did not wish their contribution to be made public. Second Muslims were concerned that in the past years state agents have been harassing Muslims and suspecting them of involvement with terror financing. In order to protect Muslim philanthropist the question "Who pays the Imam salary?" almost always raised suspicion and the respondent avoided giving direct replies in naming names or organizations.

Nevertheless local organizations like the Jamia mosque have in recent times put up advertisement in which they seek to recruit competent Imams whom they will give an at-

Imams' madrasa education

Imams in Kenya have enjoyed a limited exposure to formal secular education. Forty eight percent (48%) have not benefited from for-

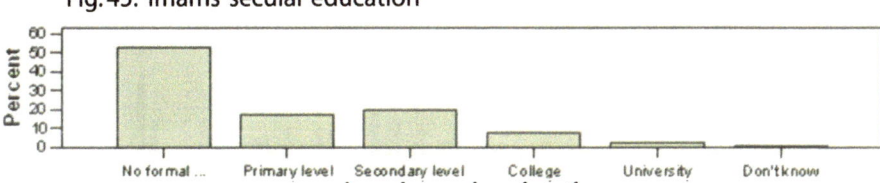

Fig. 45: Imams' secular education

mal secular schooling. A few have studied to University level. Imams with both a primary and secondary level of secular education comprised between twenty five to thirty percent (25-30%) of the totals. Some ten percent (10%) of Imams have attained some college level (post-secondary, but not university) of secular education.

Generally, levels of *madrasa* education attained by most Imams' were surprisingly low. Most Imams attained *mutawasit* level which corresponds to a mid-level educational qualification just after the basic *ibtidai* (secondary

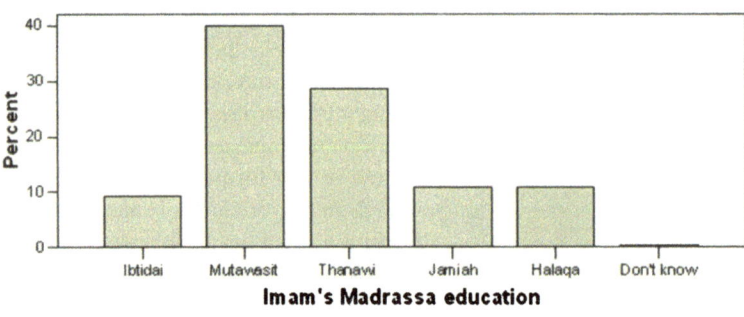

Fig. 46: Imam's madrasa education

level). The *thanawi* (post secondary not university level) was the knowledge level of about twenty five percent (25 %) of the Imams in Kenya.

Between ten and twelve percent (10-12%) of Imams in Kenya had attained *jamiah* or university levels. It is worthwhile noting that a significant percentage of Imams did not acquire their knowledge through institutions but were instructed by individuals renowned for their piety and religious learning. The category of Imams who have acquired knowledge through the *halaqa* comprises about ten percent (10%) of the Imams in Kenya. The existence of *halaqa* as a form of training for Imams corresponds to regions that have extensive traditions of Islamic learning which have produced competent individuals able to instruct others either on the verandah of their homesteads or some 'corners of mosques' in their *darsa*.

The graph below indicates that Imams on the Coast fall into all categories of *madrasa* education but a significant majority, about sixty five percent (65%) learned through *halaqa*. Slightly above ten percent (10%) of the Imams in Coast Province had attained *jamiah* levels while fifty eight percent (58%) had a basic level of *ibtidai*. Imams from Eastern Province cut across all levels of *madrasa* learning.

What is striking about North Eastern Province is the high percentage of university trained Imam's compared to other levels. About forty five percent (45%) of Imams in North Eastern Province attended Islamic university. Except for Nairobi which also has

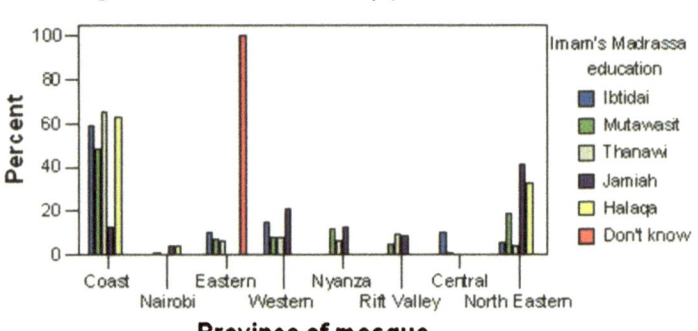

Fig. 47: Imam's education by province

university level Imams other provinces were served by Imams who had mostly basic levels of *madrasa* learning. The most common Islamic institutions where Imams attained university levels of education include Islamic universities in Kuwait and Madina, Saudi Arabia.

However most Imams are trained locally having finished their *madrasa* education in local institutions. The College of Islamic Studies in Kisauni, north of Mombasa, Riyadha Mosque College in Lamu and the Mambrui

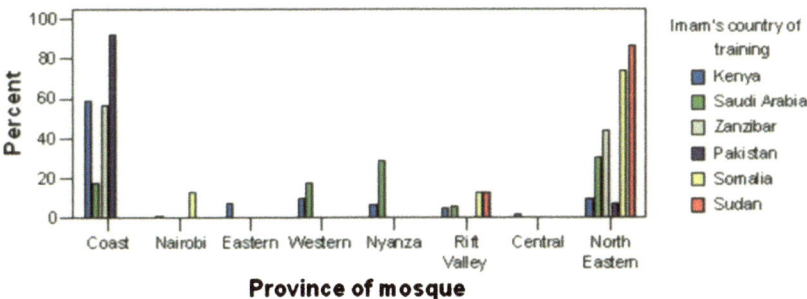

Fig. 48: Country of Imam's training by province

madrasa are the main local institutions that have produced most of the locally trained Imams. All provinces have the majority of its Imams locally trained. However, Imams trained in some countries tend to concentrate in specific regions. For example, Nyanza Province has most Imams trained in Saudi Arabia, while Nairobi has most Imams who are trained in Somalia. Imams trained in Pakistan are few and mostly concentrated in the Coast and Nairobi Province.

Does the level of secular and *madrasa* training influence in any way the articulation of Islamic knowledge and approaches where Imams debate religious and social issues? The survey sought for Muslim opinions on this based on their perception of the *khutba*.

Khutba and policy

Muslims characterized Imams as vocal, likewise agreed to a large extent that the content of the *khutba* given by Imams addressed social and political matters. During the survey most of what Muslims consider the political contents in the *khutba* had to do with the fact that Imams had discussed issues concerning the *kadhi* courts in the constitution and the referendum on adoption of a new constitution.

It was evident during the debate on the constitution that Imams influenced how Muslims voted in the referendum. In fact the CIPK opposed the draft constitution and influenced a majority of Muslims to hold that view. However, forty percent (40%) of Muslims did not hear the *khutba* as addressing policy matters but between ten to fifteen percent (10%-15%) of Muslims agreed 'very strongly' that policy was discussed by Imams in their sermons. Since between forty to forty five percent (40%-45%) agreed that Imams' sermons addressed policy matters, the conclusion is that the majority of Muslims perceive *khutba* given by Imams to contain strong views and discussion bearing on policy matters.

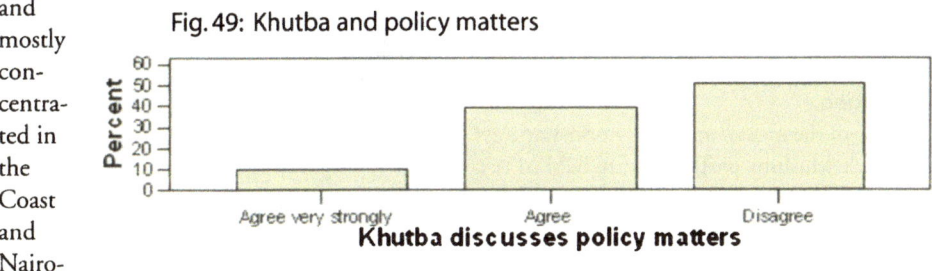

Fig. 49: Khutba and policy matters

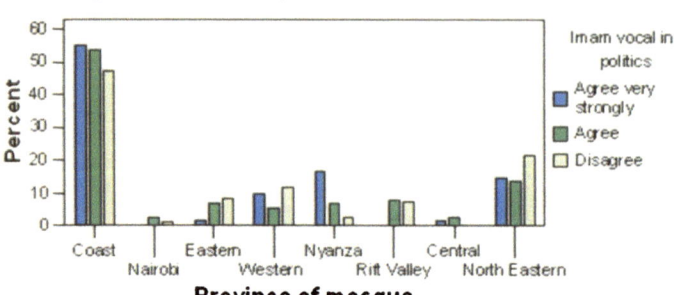

Fig. 50: Imams and politics

Muslims in Kenya are generally active in politics. The majorities of Muslims have participated in some political demonstration before and will be ready to participate in them in the future. Eighty percent (80%) of respondents said they were always active in political demonstrations. Nevertheless, a few, comprising eighteen percent (18%) of the total survey population, said that they would 'sometimes' participate. Muslims who have had little participation in political demonstrations comprised four percent (4%) of the survey population.

Some of the most common demonstrations in which Muslims participate are held in response to local events including claims by Muslims of police harassment and anti-terrorism legislations. At the same time international events have also elicited Muslims reaction in the form of demonstrations that included the burning of flags. Examples of such activities are Muslims anti-war demonstrations against the Israel invasion of Lebanon, an the American and British invasion of Iraq and Afghanistan.

Fig. 51: Muslims protesting against invasion of Iraq and Afghanistan

Imams and politics in the mosques

Muslims who attend the *khutba* at the mosque were asked to characterize the contents of their Imam's sermon by explaining their feelings on the *khutba* political content. The majority of Muslims in Kenya consider Imams' sermons to

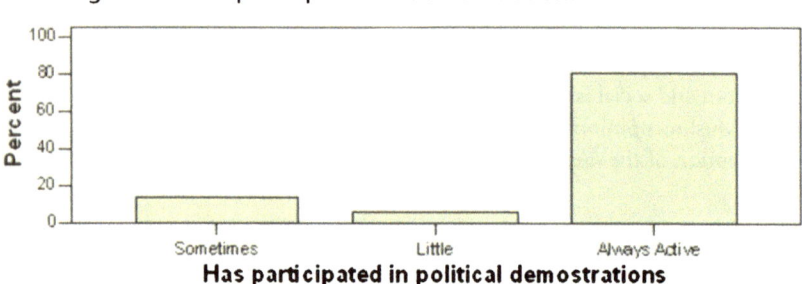

Fig. 52: Muslim participation in demonstrations

contain radical political elements and thought that Imams were vocal in their discussion of political matters.

Responses to the statement 'Imams are vocal in politics' resulted in about forty percent (40%) disagreeing; the remaining sixty percent (60%) agreed that Imam's were vocal when addressing political matters before their audiences. Out of the majority who agreed, twenty eight percent (28%) strongly agreed and thought that characterizing Imams' as vocal political commentators represented the true political position of Imams. Another thirty two percent (32%) simply agreed but did not emphasize a strong resonance to the statement.

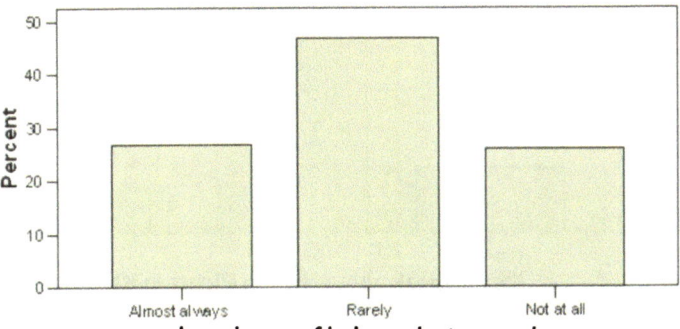

Fig. 53: Imams and independent reasoning (ra'y)

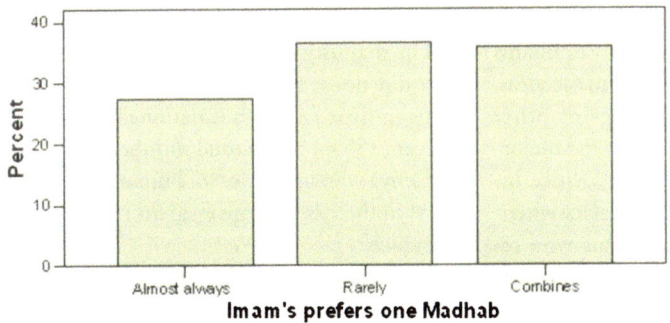

Fig. 54: Imam's preference for single madhhab

The feeling that Imams are vocal in politics was most notable in the fifty five percent (55%) of Muslims polled in Coast Province. An almost equally high ratio, forty five percent (45%) of the survey, respondents from the Coast likewise held the opinion that Imams are not vocal in politics. The majority of Muslims in Nyanza Province concur that Imams are vocal. In North Eastern Province the majority of respondents disagreed with the statement that Imams were vocal political commentators. Asked to explain this phenomenon one Muslim respondent from North Eastern Province had this to say "this province has many political problems, Imams try to address them but they haven't done enough, we need to hear more on politics from the learned Muslims who are Imams."[2]

Generally, Muslims thought *khutba* given at mosques contains vocal political messages but they did not think that Imams espoused particularly original and innovative ideas in their *khutba*.

Forty eight percent (48%) of imams rarely used independent reasoning (*ra'y*) while delivering the *khutba*. Twenty-eight percent

---

2) *Comments extracted from a focused group discussion in Mandera.*

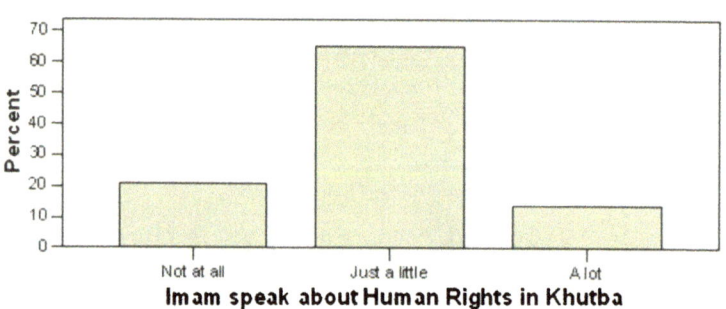

Fig. 55: Imams speaking about human rights

(28%) of Imams felt they were always innovative in their *khutba* and almost always used *ra'y*. Another twenty eight percent (28%) of Imams said they did not attempt any *ra'y* in their *khutba*. Given that Imams rarely used *ra'y* then the practice of *taqlid* appeared widespread. Fifty percent (50%) of Imam's almost always made reference to ideas and thoughts from other scholars in their *khutba*. Imams who rarely made reference to other scholars comprised forty percent (40%) of the survey while those who did not at all include the teachings of other scholars in their *khutba* comprised ten percent (10%) of the Imams.

In the Coast Province the majority of Imams will 'almost always' make reference to the ideas, thoughts opinions and teachings of other scholars in their *khutba*. Similarly, the majority of Imams in North Eastern Province included the opinions of other scholars whenever they made the *khutba*. Imams who responded with 'not at all' to the use of other scholars' teachings in their *khutba* comprised the majority of those polled in Western, Nyanza and Rift Valley Provinces.

The majority of Kenyan Muslims are Sunni of the Shafii *madhhab*. But the survey indicates that Imams are divided between using the predominantly Shafii *madhhab* and including the opinions of other schools of *fiqh* in their *khutba* or *darsa*. Thirty five percent (35%) of Imams rarely use other *madhhab* in their articulation of *fiqh* principles; perhaps another thirty five percent (35%) will combine *madhhab* when faced with matters of *fiqh*. Another twenty five percent (25%) will 'almost always' use teachings from one *madhhab*.

Imams and socio-political issues

Muslims felt that Imams' *khutba* did not adequately address issues concerning human rights. Sixty two percent (62%) of Muslims thought that the content of human rights issues in Imams' *khutba* was 'just a little'. Twenty percent (20%) did 'not at all' include human right contents in the *khutba*. Ten percent (10%) of Imams had 'a lot' of human right content in their *khutba*.

The majority of Imams in the Coast Province did 'not at all' include human rights contents in their *khutba* but nationally, fifty five percent (55%) of the total number of Imams in Kenya who used 'a lot' of human right contents in their *khutba* are resident in the Coast Province.

In North Eastern Province, Imams who used human rights content in their *khutba* were the majority. The majority of Imams in Western, Nyanza, and Rift Valley used 'just a little' human rights content in their *khutba*. But why don't Muslim Imams discuss human rights? In one of the focused group discussions with Imams, Imam B gave us his opinions on why this was the case. First was his disagreement with the definition of what constitutes the main topics of human rights. These appear to influence the Imam's inclusion and exclusion of the subject in the *khutba*. For Imam B it appears that a discussion of human rights had to focus on rights of women, veils, female genital mutilations (FGM) all of which are topics that target Islam for condemnation. For this reason Imam B thought that he could not participate in condemning Islam in the name of addressing human rights. Imam B felt that human rights are a topic always defined by non-Muslims whose interests are to condemn Islam. Imam B felt that a discussion of police harassment of Muslims and arbitrary arrest of Muslims by the anti-terrorism police unit is a violation of human rights. However, according to Imam B any Muslims who include such criticism of the conduct of state agents are accused of supporting terrorism but not addressing the issue of human rights.[3]

Fig. 56: Friday Bulletin on arrest of Muslims

off from Moi International Airport, Mombasa.

In 2003, the government published the Suppression of Terrorism Bill. Muslims found the bill objectionable on grounds that its provisions violated the constitution and would lead to abuses of human rights. Muslim leaders are particularly concerned that the bill targets the community for profiling. In 2004 the CIPK accused the government of harassing Muslim and prematurely applying the bill before it become law when thirty Muslims were arrested on terrorism charges. Although the state backed off from its initial attempts its continued intention to revive the bill are seen by Muslims as attempts by foreign government to influence the state and institutionalize discrimination against Muslims. Even as Muslim challenge the bill the states reaction to these incidents has been to target Muslims for arbitrary arrests; attempts to re-enact the draconian anti-terrorism law and the establishment of an anti-terrorism police unit. Muslims have reacted in the form

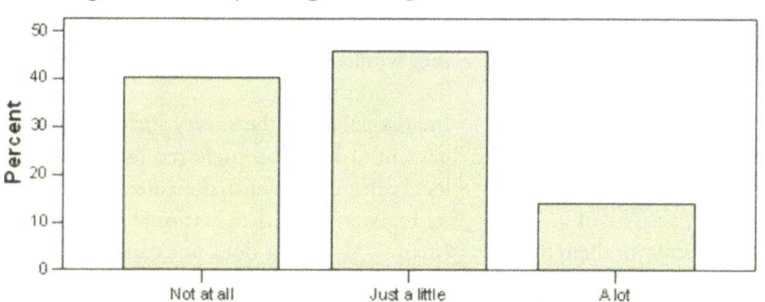

Fig. 57: Imams speaking on dangers of terrorism

Addressing terrorism

Three local incidents define the concern over terrorism in Kenya; the bombing of the American Embassy in downtown Nairobi during August 1998; burning down of a tourist resort at Kikambala along the coast of Kenya a few years later and an alleged attempt to shoot down a passenger flight while taking

---

3) *Extracts from a focus group discussion with Imam B (not real name) in Western Province.*

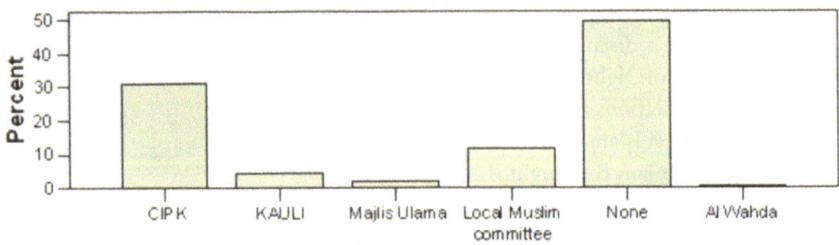

Fig. 58: Imams membership to networks

of protest and demonstrations against the proposed anti-terrorism legislation and against the anti-terrorism police unit. In their complaints Muslims accuse state agencies, especially the anti-Terrorism police unit, of targeting them for cultural profiling and mistreatment.

We asked Muslims to characterize how often Imams in their mosques discussed the dangers of terrorism in the *khutba*. Forty percent (40%) thought that their Imams did 'not at all' discuss the dangers of terrorism in their *khutba*. A slightly high percentage of forty-five (45%) thought that Imams discussed dangers of terrorism but 'just a little'. A minority of ten percent (10%) thought discussions on the dangers of terrorism amongst Imams was 'a lot'. Muslims felt that while terrorism was in itself an abomination, the fact that Muslims were always generally accused of supporting terrorism made it difficult for them to gain the courage to have an open discussion on the topic. But the important point to note is that discussions occur in reaction to arrest of suspected Muslim. In most cases Muslims discuss the injustices committed in the act of arrests but not the general dangers real or imagined of the acts of terrorism.

Imams' networks

The important role played by Imams in Muslim society has led to attempts at organization by creating networks. These are expected to be forums where matters of mutual concerns to the Imams and the general wellbeing of Muslims in Kenya are channeled for discussion. Through these networks Imams are expected to give directions and advice to Muslims The most prominent *ulama* networks include the Council of Imams and Preachers of Islam in Kenya (CIPK), the Majlis Ulama, Kenya Assembly of Ulama in Islam (KAULI), and Al-Wahda. The latter is a new outfit formed by *madrasa* teachers who add to their teaching duties with leading prayers in some mosques. In areas where Muslims have not joined the widely known *ulama* networks they would belong to a number of local Muslim committees.

Imams polled in the survey include thirteen percent (13%) who preferred to belong to a local committee within their areas as opposed to registering with a national network of Imams. Al-Wahda does not consider itself a network of *ulama* or Imams but that of *madrasa* teachers; fifty percent (50%) of Imams were members of this network. The most known national *ulama* network, the CIPK, had about twenty seven percent (27%) following amongst mosque Imams interviewed for this survey. During the duration that data was collected a new *ulama* network, the Majlis Ulama had recently come into existence for a few months. About eight percent (8%) of Imams claimed membership to the Majlis Ulama. An analysis of the distribution of membership of Imams in various networks in the provinces found that the CIPK had a strong following in the Coast Province where about fifty eight percent (58%) of Imams were members.

Yet, eighty five percent (85%) of Imams in the Coast Province were also members of local committees. Imams who belonged to a local Muslim committee as opposed to the main *ulama* network concentrated in the North Eastern Province, Rift Valley and Coast Province.

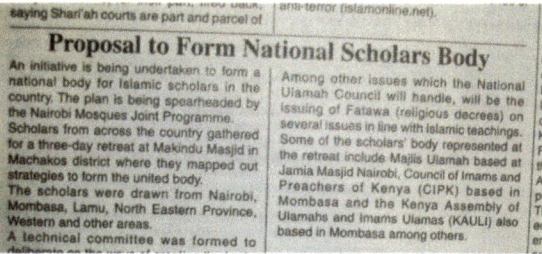

Fig. 59: Proposal to form national body of Muslim scholars

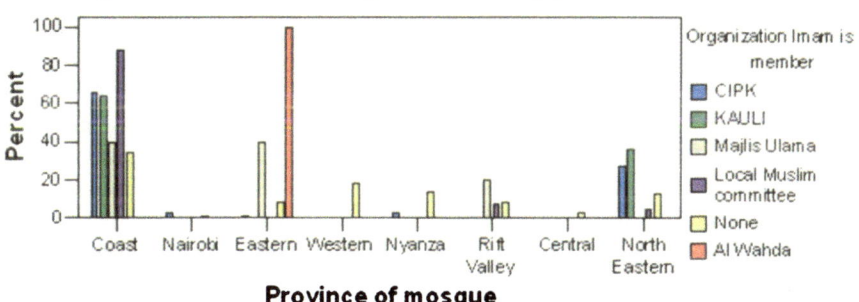

Fig. 60: Imams membership to networks by province

SECTION FIVE

Muslims and politics

Muslims' participation in politics in Kenya is a much talked about topic. Because of their minority status, Muslims have made a significant impact perhaps more than expected of a minority population. There have been Muslims elected to parliament since independence, of late some have held high profile ministerial position, nevertheless few Muslims can be considered to have created a niche to be national figures.

In this survey we explored Muslims' opinions on a variety of questions especially those with a bearing on Muslim political ambitions, views and inclinations. First, was the question on whether Muslims consider it their national duty to take active roles in national politics? Muslims were asked to give responses to this question because of the constant complaints that politics in Kenya was conducted based on Christian principles resulting in discrimination and political marginalization of Muslims. In fact during early 2006 prominent personalities were encouraging Muslims to play an active role in all political processes in Kenya.[4]

Thus, in March-July when the survey was undertaken, fifty five percent (55%) of Muslims strongly agreed that it is a duty for Muslims to participate in politics, twenty eight percent (28%) were hesitant but nevertheless willing to participate, while seventeen percent

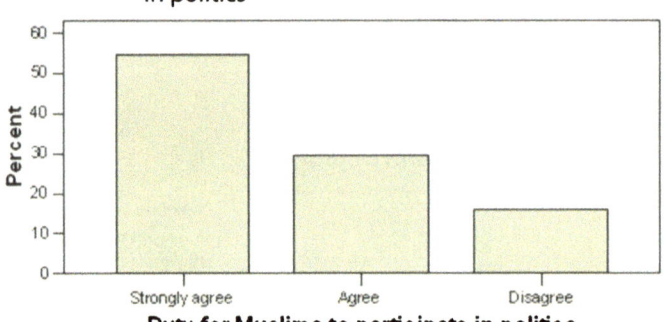

Fig. 61: Muslim attitudes towards participation in politics

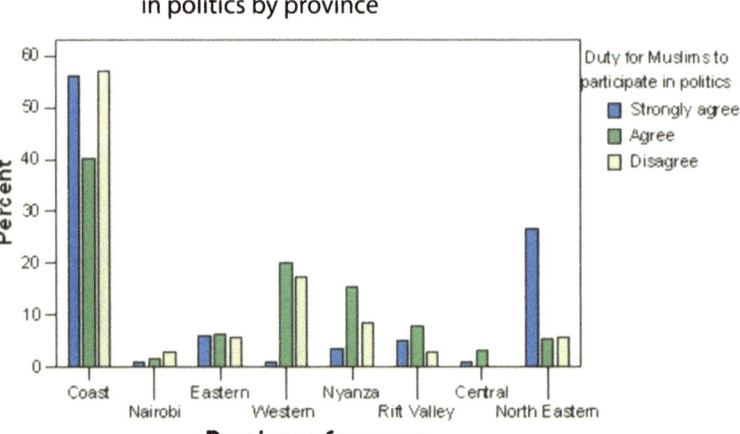

Fig. 62: Muslim attitudes towards participation in politics by province

---

4) See *The Friday Bulletin* January 27, 2006.

Muslims and freedom of worship

Levels of religious tolerance in Kenya were generally high. There have been cases where state agents especially the police have been accused of desecrating Muslims' places of worship when entered mosques with the boots in pursuit of criminals suspected of hiding in the mosques. Prior to the bombing of the American Embassy in Nairobi during August 1998 there was very little state-Muslim engagement that could have been interpreted as interference with Muslims' freedom of worship. From thence on suspicion towards Muslims has heightened. The situation

> **Involve more in Politics, Muslims advised**
> Calls are growing urging Muslims to increase their participation in the political process as a way of bringing the community from the throttles of discrimination and marginalization.
> A former commissioner with the Constitutional of Kenya Review Commission (CKRC) Sheikh Ibrahim Lethome said that last year's referendum results demonstrated that with active participation in the country's political arena, the Muslim community can be an influential block in national matters. He said the power of the Muslim vote could be used to demand for the rights of Muslims which are being constantly trampled upon.
> He also urged the community to be conscious of the rights due to them as citizens of this country and alluded that many were facing discrimination and oppression due to ignorance of their constitutional rights.
> Sheikh Lethome was speaking at an induction seminar for human rights defenders and monitors in Nairobi at the weekend. The one-day seminar was organized by the Muslim Human Rights Forum
> *Continued To Page 4*

(17%) thought that Kenyan politics were not favorable to Islam and Muslims; these showed a preference to decline or disagree about participation in politics.

Most Muslims who disagree with participation in politics reside in the Coast Province. About fifty five percent (55%), of the total respondents in the national survey who disagreed are coastal Muslims. However fifty percent (50%) of the total population of Muslims in the Coast Province agreed and were willing to participate in politics. Above is a caption from the Friday Bulletin encouraging Muslims to participate more in politics. Twenty two percent (22%) of the total ratio of Muslims who agree to participate in politics are from Western Kenya. Muslims from North Eastern Province constitute thirty percent (30%) of those who strongly agree about participation in politics. In Central Province Muslim were few but mostly favored active participation.

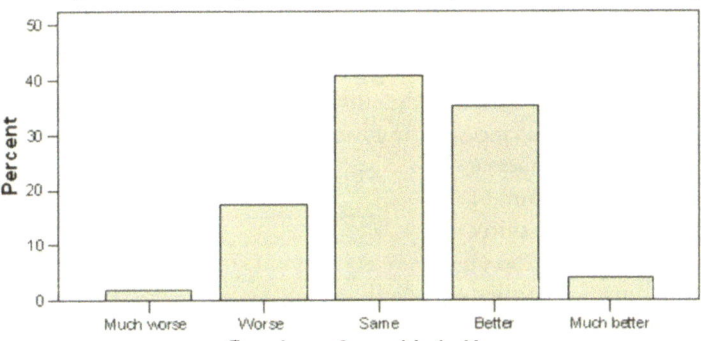

Fig. 64: Muslim opinion on availability of freedom of worship

worsened after 9-11 as the government was constantly accused of harassing Muslims in its attempts to arrest people suspected of engaging in terror. A local scenario like the debate on the draft constitution has shown that inter-religious animosities can easily be inflamed in Kenya with implications for the extent at which Muslim freedom of worship can be elastic. Muslims accuse the state of hostility. Flimsy excuses like the fight against terrorism has been used by state agencies like the police and immigration department to harass Muslims who go to their offices to ask for essential documents like passports and national identity cards.

Because state authorities rigorously scrutinize and question those with Muslim names, there is a general opinion that the state does not respect the freedoms and rights of Muslims. During the period of the survey Muslims did not see changes in the government's attitudes and practice towards freedom of worship. About thirty eight percent (38%) of Muslims polled thought that the state of freedom of worship in Kenya was the same, slightly below, about thirty six percent (36%), were of the opinion that freedom of worship had improved, while nine percent (9%) of Muslims were impressed and said that freedom of worship had improved and was much better. Nevertheless, twenty percent (20%) of Muslims were not satisfied and thought that the conditions for freedom of worship were worse.

Muslims' perception on freedom of worship in Kenya varies by province. In North Eastern Province Muslims showed a pronounced negative perception on the availability of freedom of worship in Kenya. Fifty five percent (55%) of those who thought freedom of worship was worse in Kenya were residents of North Eastern Province. Meanwhile, fifty five percent (55%) of Muslims who thought freedom of worship was much better were polled from Coast Province. In the Rift Valley, Muslims ranked freedom of worship between worse and better, ten percent (10%) of Muslims thought freedom of worship was the same, eight percent (8%) thought it was worse, while a few Muslims, five percent (5%) of those polled in Rift Valley, were of the opinion that conditions of freedom of worship were better.

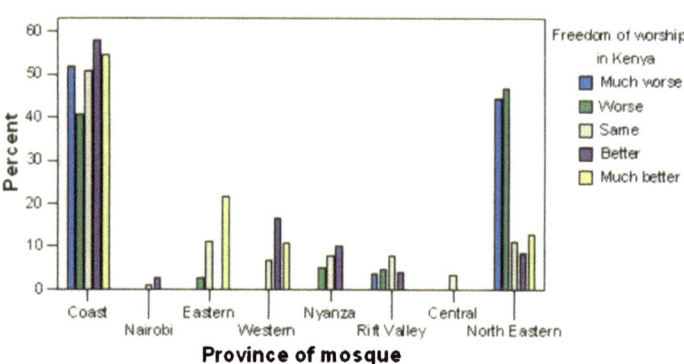

Fig. 65: Muslim opinion on availability of freedom of worship by province

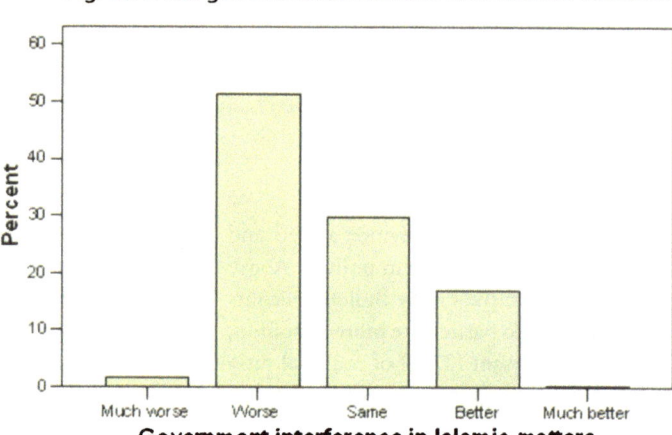

Fig. 66: Does government interfere with Islamic matters?

In response to the query 'Does government interfere in Islamic matters?' the general attitude was that of dissatisfaction. Muslims think the government performed badly and has interfered in Islamic matters. Fifty nine percent (59%) of Muslims thought the government's interference on Islamic matters was worse, while twelve percent (12%) thought the government has improved and showed less interference. A significant twenty nine percent (29%) said that government continued interfering in Islamic matters.

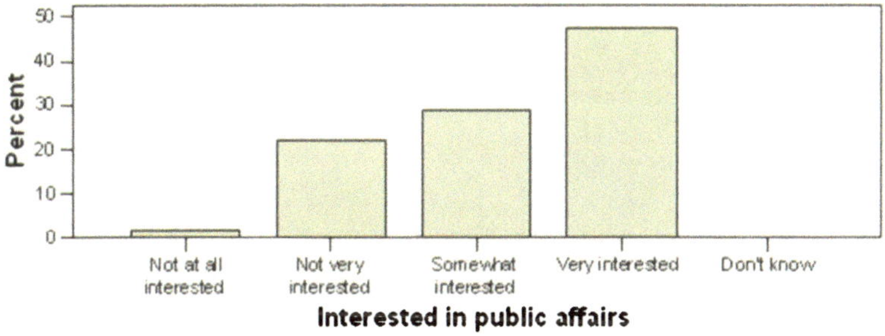

Generally, the majority of Muslims thought of themselves as politically active, concerned and interested in public affairs. These were Muslims who had a habit of attending public *baraza*, school meetings, security meetings, or stopped to inquire when a neighbors raised an alarm or have presented a petition to the local council requesting it to address specific matters. Forty three percent (43%) of Muslims said they were very interested and keen on public affairs, while twenty six percent (26%) were interested but less active. About twenty percent (20%) of Muslims who responded to this survey did not show interest in public affairs.

Fig. 67: Muslim interest in public affairs

Interest in public affairs shown by Muslims varied in accordance to the province. Skepticism towards public affairs was prevalent amongst Muslims in Coast Province where about sixty percent (60%) considered themselves not interested in public affairs; those who thought they were somewhat interested accounted for about thirty eight percent (38%).

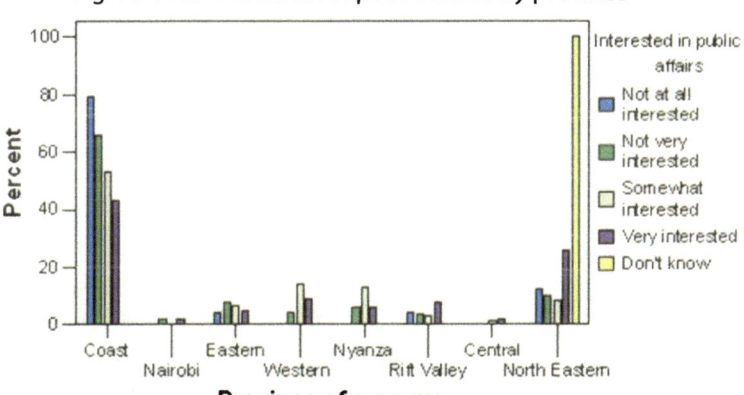

Fig. 68: Muslim interest in public affairs by province

Muslims who were actively concerned about public affairs made up thirty three percent (32%) of Muslims in the Coast Province.

The majority of Muslims in North Eastern Province considered themselves very interested in public affairs. Twenty three percent (23%) of those polled in the survey were Muslims

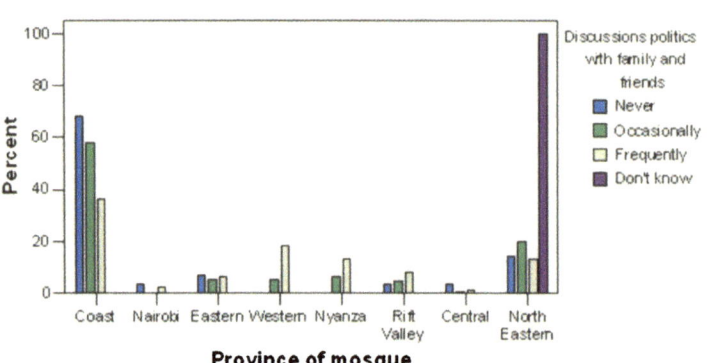

Fig. 69: How often Muslims discuss politics by province

occasionally a habit of about fifty percent (50%) of Muslims. Thirty five percent (35%) frequently discussed politics with family and friends while ten percent (10%) never engaged their friends and family in any political discussions.

In the previous charts we showed how the largest percentage of Muslims in Coast Province were least interested in public affairs. Similarly Muslims in Coast Province did not make it a habit to discuss politics with friends and family. About fifty nine percent (59%) in the national survey who did not discuss politics with family and friends were Muslims in Coast Province; they never engage family and friends in political discussions. When separated by province, fifty one percent (51%) of Muslims in the Coast Province 'occasionally' discussed politics with friends and family. Meanwhile, twenty six percent (26%) of Muslims in the Coast Province frequently held

from North Eastern Province who participate actively and took an interest in public affairs. Nairobi province did not contribute a large percentage of Muslims selected in the survey, but Muslims from Nairobi were categorical they were either 'not interested' or 'interested'. There were no Muslims in Nairobi who thought of their concern in public affairs as 'somewhat interested'. The majority of Muslims who polled somewhat interested in public affairs were from Western and Nyanza Provinces. In each of these provinces the category 'somewhat interested' was responded to by the highest percentage of people.

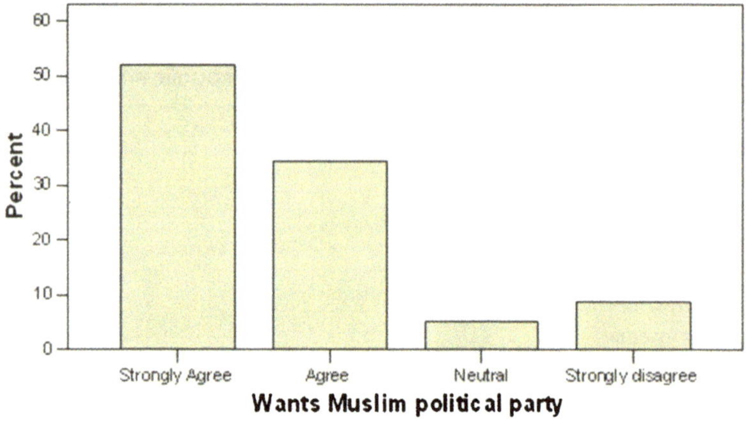

Interest shown by Muslims in public affairs also reflected on the habit of Muslim people of discussing politics with family and friends. The survey found out that a political discussion between friends and family members was

Fig. 70: Should Muslims register a political party

political discussions with friends and family. The majority of Muslims in Western Province and Nyanza frequently engaged in political discussion. The survey shows that the majority of Muslims in Nyanza and Western Provinces engaged and discussed politics; none indicated they never discussed politics.

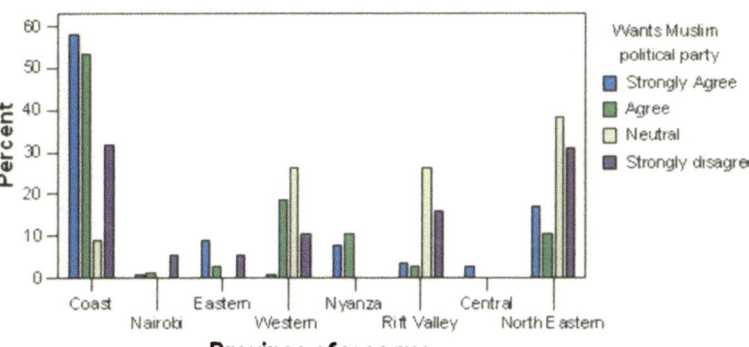

Fig. 71: Muslims attitudes towards registering a political party by province

Idea of an Islamic political party

In the 1990s Kenya experienced what has been called the second liberation; a period that refers to the opening up of the political landscape through a re-introduction of multi-party politics. This aspect of 'social engineering' created an opportunity for Muslims who attempted to register a party, the Islamic Party of Kenya (IPK) in 1992. A protracted legal challenge was mounted based on the constitutionality of registering a party based on a religious affiliation. The religiosity of IPK was rather ambiguous. A glimpse at IPK's constitution documents reveals the ambiguity of its religious base. For example Section 3.1.1 states its objectives as to serve as a political party committed to the establishment and maintenance of a God conscious constitutional government', Section 3.1.2 state its modus operandi as 'to be a consultative, democratic, and just political movement that shall seek to transform the people into a strong willed, morally and socially committed and tolerant nation that values justice, peace, democracy, unity, love, cooperation and participation of all Kenya in national development.'[5] It is clear that IPK documents described its philosophy as secular although its name and following was largely comprised of Muslims. IPK had most of its strong following from Mombasa and other districts of the Coast Province. IPK was denied registration and its status has remained as such. The name 'Islamic' might led one to assume the foundation of IPK to be much closer to an expression of a national Muslims consciousness. Indeed such ideas might have some ground and the attorney general stated that the party was denied registration because it was based on religion, contrary to the constitution. However, Muslims see it as essentially a non-sectarian movement which stresses civil rights and human rights with a unique reference to Islamic principles. The fact that IPK has been denied legal status has hampered its activities but its officials continue to carry on using their original designations, when they issue a statement it is recorded as 'so and so... of the unregistered IPK'.

Despite IPK's lack of registration the sur-

---

5) *Constitution of the Islamic Party of Kenya, February 7, 1992.*

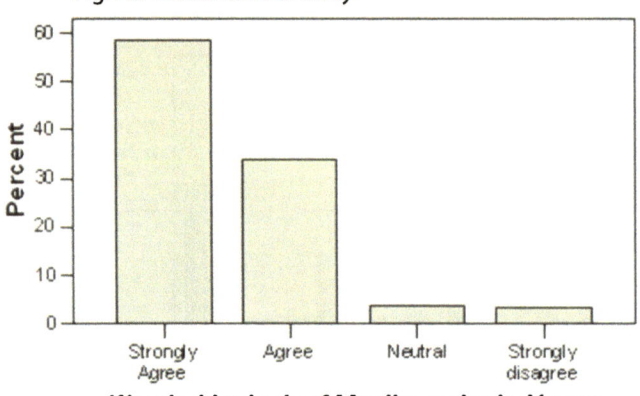

Worried by lack of Muslim unity in Kenya

Fig. 72: Muslims and unity

vey found that the idea of a Muslim political party still resonates with Muslims in Kenya. A majority of Muslims were in favor of establishing a Muslim political party to champion Muslims' political interests. Close to seventy five percent (75%) of respondents to this survey were strongly in favor of establishing a Muslim political party in Kenya. About ten percent (10%) of Muslims thought it was not a good idea and disagreed with the suggestion to establish a Muslim political party while five percent (5%) are undecided and choose to remain 'neutral' on the idea.

In the provinces the idea received varied responses but the majority of Muslims in the Coast Province strongly agreed to the establishment of a Muslim political party. The majority of Muslims in Western, Nyanza, Rift Valley, and North Eastern Province took a neutral position. A minority of Muslims in Central Province responded to the question but the majority of these were strongly in favor of the establishment of a Muslim political party.

Mosques, politicians and political leadership

The relationship between mosques and politicians is ambivalent and we asked mosque participants to express how well they regard the role played by Muslims politicians in articulating their problems and finding solutions to some of them.

The general perception amongst Muslims was that the population was not united in purpose and this tendency was worrying to the majority of Muslims. In fact this perception was purportedly strongly held by fifty six percent

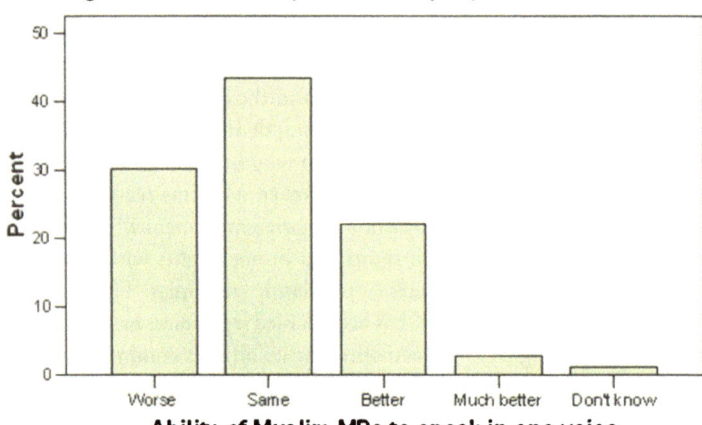

Fig. 73: Muslims and parliamentary representation

Ability of Muslim MPs to speak in one voice

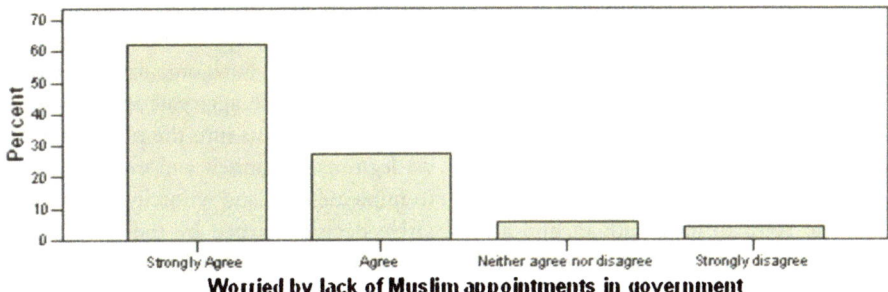

Fig. 74: Appointment of Muslims by government

(56%) of the respondents, another thirty seven percent (37%) agreed that lack of Muslim unity worried them while four percent (4%) thought that the problem of Muslim unity did not matter to them and these opted to remain neutral. There were Muslims who were not worried at all, and these strongly disagreed with the notion that lack of Muslim unity was a matter of concern to them. Apart from lack of unity Muslims were particularly concerned that less and less Muslims were occupying high offices in the government compared to adherents of other religions.

Muslims' concerns about lack of unity are further emphasized by their concern that Muslim people elected to parliament usually do not speak in unison about matters affecting the Muslim population.

Most Muslims thought that Muslims' lack of unity in parliament would remain the same, twenty five percent (25%) of the selected interviewers thought that the situation would improve and become better, about thirty percent (30%) thought that it would worsen and Muslim MPs would continue to show lack of unity in parliament while a small fraction two percent (2%) of the population in the survey,

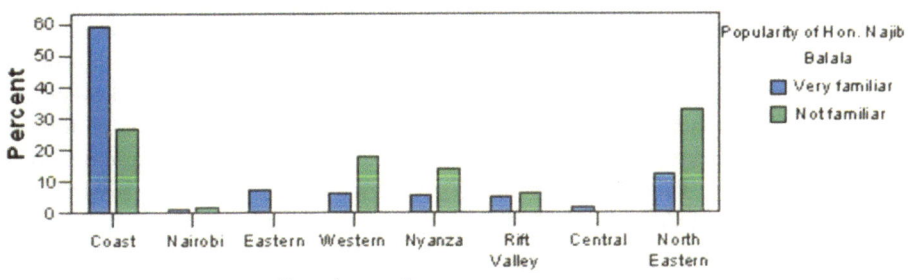

Fig. 75: Popular politician

were optimistic that the situation would improve.

Again, a majority of Muslims, sixty percent (60%), expressed their strongest concern on the lack of Muslim appointments to high offices in government, yet another significant twenty eight percent (28%) agreed with the concern while those who choose to remain neutral comprised about five percent (5%). Another five percent (5%) did not have this concern.

The survey also probed Muslim perceptions of Muslim MPs who were in high profile offices during the period of the survey. These included Hon. Najib Balala and Hon. Chirau Ali Mwakwere; both held ministerial positions. The survey wanted to find out the political appeal these politicians held across the Muslim population in Kenya.

Muslims polled in this survey were familiar with Hon. Najib Balala and seventy eight percent (78%) seem to have faith in him as a Muslim leader. About twenty two percent (22%) of the survey population said that Hon. Najib Balala was not familiar to them.

When the survey was conducted Hon. Balala was one of the ODM luminaries who had campaigned against the proposed draft constitution in the referendum and eventually contributed to the draft constitution being rejected by Kenyans including a majority of Muslims.

Hon. Balala's popularity varied in the provinces. He was considered familiar and popular by a majority in his native Coast Province, but still about twenty five percent (25%) of Muslims in the Coast Province did not consider Hon. Balala a familiar politician. The majority of Muslims in North Eastern were categorical that Hon. Balala was unfamiliar to them. A similar situation where Muslims in the majority thought that Hon. Balala was not familiar was evident in Nyanza and Western Provinces.

All Muslims polled in Eastern Province categorized Hon. Balala as familiar to them. Certainly this distribution of Hon. Balala's familiarity in the provinces where the survey was carried out pointed to Hon. Balala's ambitions to vie for presidency through nomination in the ODM-Kenya party being realistic.

Muslim organizations

There have been several attempts at achieving some genuinely collective representation of Kenyan Muslims partly initiated by the Muslims themselves, partly by the state. The state obviously preferred an organization which was representative enough to count as 'the Muslim organization'. Such organizations was expected to articulate, aggregate and channel the interest of Muslims into the political system via legitimate channels and even contribute to implementing and enforcing the authoritative decisions taken by the state thereby maintaining political stability and reflecting the governments legitimacy. Yet the organization was not expected to be so independent as to challenge the state. Therefore contribution to the political public space has been articulated by a number of groups who have assumed for themselves tags of 'Muslims mouthpieces'. The first attempt at collective representation was the National Union of Kenya Muslims (NUKEM) which was established in 1968. Groups like the NUKEM, and the Supreme Council of Kenya Muslims (SUPKEM) have been in existence for decades. The NUKEM was established in Mombasa with aims amongst others of the improvement of Muslim social and economic conditions. NUKEM is one of the oldest and amongst the first Muslim association to attempt to unite Muslim welfare groups into one umbrella body. In the 1970s NUKEM's influence was superseded by that of SUPKEM which came into existence in 1973. SUPKEM was established to enhance the capacity of Muslims to articulate their development concerns, in a joint forum. During its formative period SUPKEM specifically acted as a 'clearing house' for local Muslim associations who wanted to seek developmental assistance from international Muslim aid groups especially from the Middle East. Over the decades SUPKEM's mandate has gone through a metamorphosis from a Muslim social development 'clearing house' to a vibrant Muslim group whose claim to be the mouthpiece representative of Muslims' demands to be has taken seriously now than before. When it came into existence SUPKEM appeared already tightly linked to government, indeed emphasizing the obligation of Muslims to show absolute loyalty towards the President. By 1979 SUPKEM had earned the dubious distinction in the form of recognition by the government as the sole legitimate representative of the Muslim population. Its organizational set-up was more ambitious than that of NUKEM, claiming to have district councils throughout the country. The perennial problem however, which has also haunted Kenya is how to strike a balance between, on the one hand, such authentic representation as requires independence from the state and, on the other loyalty to the state and the incumbent rulers which cannot possible be guaranteed if the organization is generally independent. Thus, SUPKEM's legitimacy among the Muslim population seems to have been questionable. In the Friday Bulletin of February 2006,[6] SUPKEM came under strong criticism for its attempt to lock out Muslims from participating in the elections of its officials by holding "secret elections". With an editorial that termed SUPKEM's intended act of holding secret elections, as "illogical, misconceived, and disrespectful to its constituency-the Muslims community,"[7] a stage was set to question the legitimacy of public officials elected in a 'secret election'. But, what is the attitude of Muslims towards such organizations?

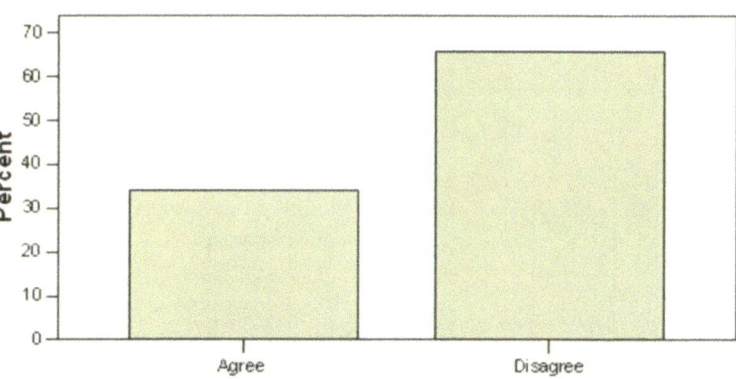

Fig. 76: Democracy in Muslim organization

Muslims are in agreement that Muslim organizations are far away from being considered democratic the manner in which they claim to represent communal interest. Only thirty two percent (32%) consider Muslim groups to be organized in accordance with democratic principles. In 2005, Muslims did not expect favorable changes in the effectiveness of Muslim organizations at the leadership level. The majority of Muslims thought it will remain the same, about thirty percent (30%) were of the opinion that leadership in Muslim organizations would become effective and hence anticipate improvement, yet another thirty percent (30%) thought situation would be 'worse' and Muslims should expect the ineffective leadership to continue.

SUPKEM

The survey investigated SUPKEM and other groups' standing in Muslim society based on these groups claims. In particular we investi-

---

1) *Friday Bulletin, Muharram 25, 1426/Feb. 24, 2006.*
2) *Friday Bulletins Editorial "SUPKEM, think twice", Issue No. 148, Muharram 25, 1426/Feb. 24, 2006.*

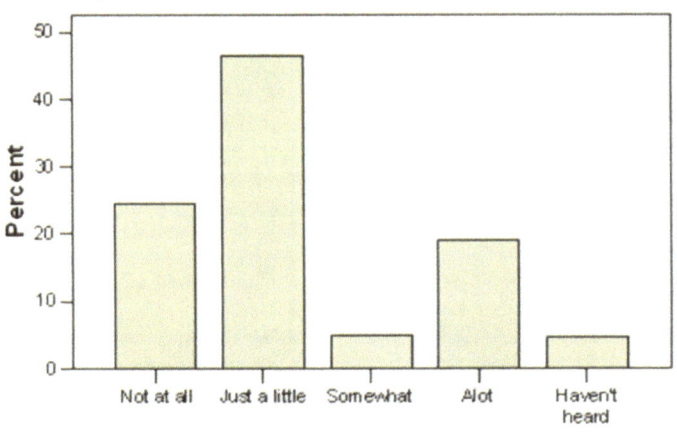

Fig. 77: SUPKEM leadership

leadership to Muslims. The majority of respondents to the survey had little faith in SUPKEM; those who responded to the question with the reply 'just a little' comprised about forty five percent (45%) of the survey population. There were pessimist in the survey population as well; these responded with 'somewhat' as

gated the perception Muslims hold about these groups "representative claims".

Muslims responded to the question "How much do you trust SUPKEM to represent Muslims?" with mixed reactions but bordering on the negative and mistrust. About twenty five percent (25%) of the survey population responded 'not at all' meaning they had no faith in SUPKEM's claims to be offering

Fig. 78: SUPKEM 'secret' elections

their perception of leadership claims by SUPKEM.

About fifteen percent (15%) of respondents were in favor of SUPKEM as a leadership institution while five percent (5%) of respondents had 'not heard' nor had no knowledge of SUPKEM's existence.

Trust in SUPKEM's leadership was unevenly spread in the provinces. The majority of Muslims in

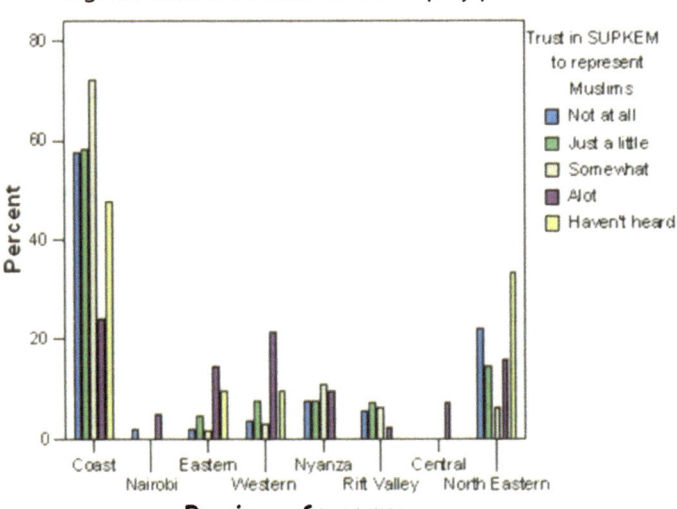

Fig. 79: Trust in SUPKEM leadership by province

North Eastern Province had not heard of SUPKEM, the second largest group is of those who did not have trust in the organization. The majority of Muslims polled in the Coast Province were pessimists; they 'somewhat' trusted SUPKEM's leadership. All Muslims polled in Central Province had a lot of trust in SUPKEM. In Eastern and Western Provinces SUPKEM had the highest percentage of Muslim's polled there indicating that they had a lot of trust in the group's leadership. In Nairobi, SUPKEM's headquarters, most Muslims polled were in favor and had 'a lot' of trust in the organization.

Council of Imams and Preachers of Islam in Kenya (CIPK)

Muslims leadership is highly contested and many times groups have emerged to make untested claims. From the 1970s such claims were the prerogative of the SUPKEM. Meanwhile SUPKEM has on several occasions attempted to incorporate the learned "fellow", the ulama into its fold. Such attempts have been difficult mainly because SUPKEM's mandate has been contested.

Fig. 80: Muslim confidence in CIPK

Trust in Council of Ulama to represent Muslims

For a long period, the ulama have been apprehensive about being included into SUPKEM. However since the year 2000 the *ulama* were able to found their own group if not to challenge SUPKEM's claims then to make one of their own.

The claims made by CIPK are also viewed with skepticism by Muslims. The majority choose to characterize their perception of CIPK's leadership as 'not at all' and 'just a little'. There was the same percentage of about twenty percent (20%) who indicated having faith in the leadership of CIPK while the same ratio had not heard or were not aware of the existence of the Council of Ulama. CIPK was in the most favorable position amongst Muslims in the North Eastern Province where the

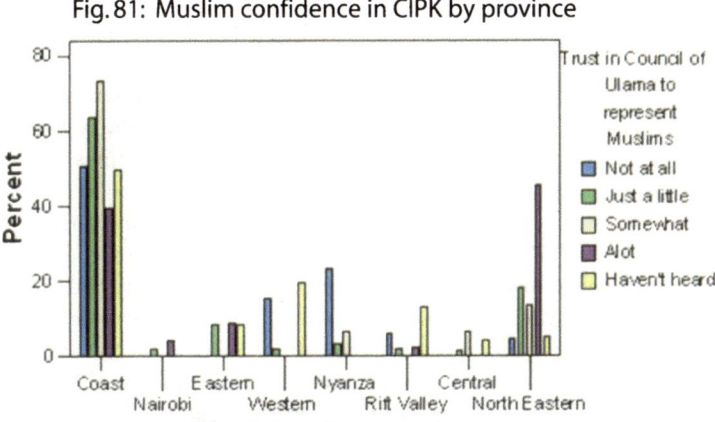

Fig. 81: Muslim confidence in CIPK by province

Fig. 82: Iqra FM

Frantic efforts to boost Iqra signal

More than a month after it moved to its new home along Ngong road, the country's pioneer Islamic radio station Iqra FM is facing erratic broadcasting problems.

Listeners have complained that its reach has narrowed significantly since it moved house from the 14th storied Bandari Plaza in Westlands. The station's signal has greatly weakened in many areas of Nairobi where it is erratic and in ⟨some⟩ areas virtually non-existing. The Central ⟨...⟩

majority of those polled had a lot of trust in CIPK's leadership.

In the Coast Province most Muslims polled said they 'somewhat' favored CIPK's leadership, the second largest group in the Coast Province had 'just a little' trust in the organization's claims to Muslims leadership. There was a significant number of Muslims in the Coast Province who had not heard about the Council of Ulama. Those who said they trust CIPK comprised about 40% of the respondents to this survey from the Coast.

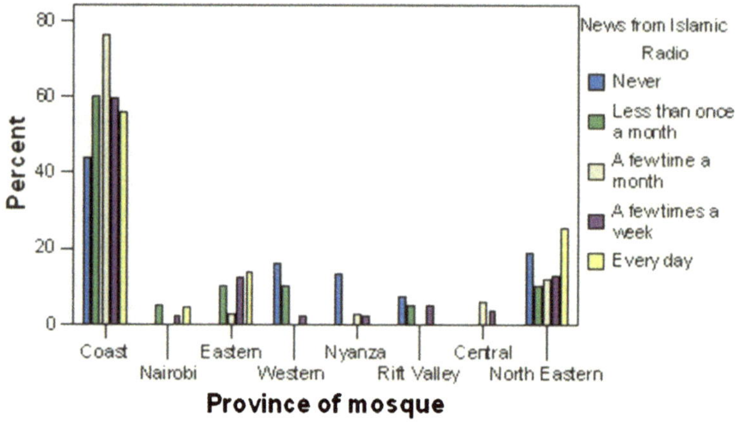

Muslim media

Since early 2000 Kenya has adopted a liberal and open policy towards access to information. The airwaves have been liberalized as radio and television mediums have frequently come into the ownership of private individuals and organizations. Muslims have taken the opportunity to apply for allocation of radio frequencies from which they operate FM Radio stations. Nairobi area was the first to be served by an Islamic radio station when Iqra FM went on air.

With programs including news analysis and varied religious program, Iqra FM provided a forum through which Muslim opinion could be shaped, but more significant, Iqra FM provided an alternative voice for Muslims. Still restricted by law to broadcast non-political content Iqra FM has nonetheless contributed significantly towards ensuring that Muslims have an avenue through which a Muslim 'message' can reach a wide listening audience.

Iqra FM's coverage is not extensive and Muslims continue to seek license to establish more Radio stations to cover wider areas.

During the period of data collection for this survey, Muslims were served by three FM stations, Iqra FM covered Nairobi and its immediate environs and Radio Rahma covered Mombasa extending to the nearby districts of Kwale, Kilifi and Malindi. Meanwhile, Radio Salam was under test awaiting broadcasting license. In North Eastern Province Muslims tuned to Star FM. We asked Muslims to determine how they use these facilities and the

Fig. 83: Muslim access to FM station

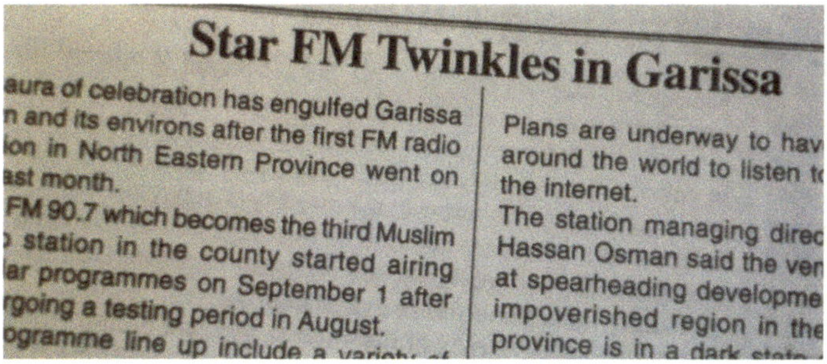
Star FM Twinkles in Garissa

aura of celebration has engulfed Garissa n and its environs after the first FM radio ion in North Eastern Province went on ast month.

FM 90.7 which becomes the third Muslim station in the county started airing ar programmes on September 1 after going a testing period in August. ogramme line up include a variety of

Plans are underway to hav around the world to listen t the internet.

The station managing direc Hassan Osman said the ver at spearheading developme impoverished region in the province is in a dark state

Fig. 84: Star FM in Garissa

results appear to suggest that only a small percentage had access to Muslim radio stations.

Forty seven percent (47%) of Muslims selected in the survey indicated they never had access to news from a Muslim radio station while forty two percent (42%) received news from a Muslim radio station only a few times in a week. Considering that the Coast Province provided a larger percentage of data and the fact that Coast Province was already served by two such radio networks including Radio Rahma (91.5 FM) and Radio Salam was under tests it can be concluded that during the period up to when the survey was conducted few Muslims had regular access to radio, especially Muslim Radio.

Fig. 85: Friday Bulletin - stories covered

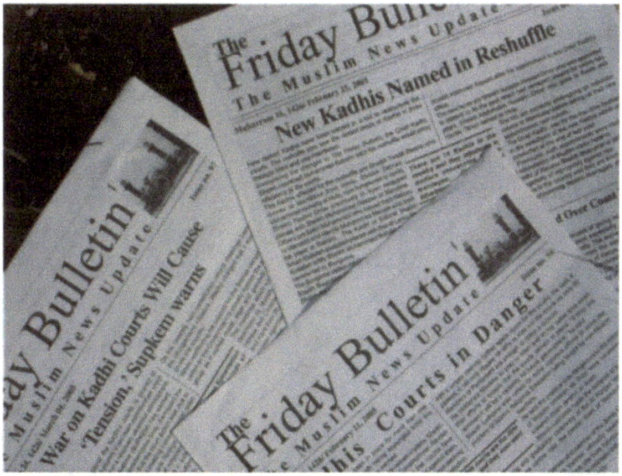

In Coast Province fifty eight percent (58%) of Muslims indicated having had access to Islamic radio a few times in a week; thirty percent (30%) said they never listen to news from Islamic radio. However, fifty five percent (55%) of respondents to the national survey said they listen and had access to Muslim radio daily were in the Coast Province. Amongst Muslims polled in Nairobi a majority said they listen to the radio daily. Muslims in Nyanza, Western and Rift Valley either 'never listened' or 'never got' news from an Islamic radio or had access to Muslim radio only a few times during the week.

Star FM (90.1) is on air in North Eastern Province where about thirty percent (30%) of Muslims had daily access to Muslim Radio, between ten to fifteen percent (10%-15%) listen to news from a Muslim radio station a few times in a week while twenty eight percent (28%) of Muslims there did not have access to Muslim radio at all. To a certain extent the reason given for this poor access to Muslim radio was not lack of broadcasting frequencies that cater for a Muslim audiences but lack of radio sets amongst most respondents.

The Television appears to be the most popular source of news and information amongst Muslims in Kenya. About forty percent (40%) had a habit of getting news and information through the Television. A further thirty five percent (35%) indicated that they watched the Television for news only a few times in a week, while about twenty percent (20%) of Muslims polled never listen or got to news through the TV.

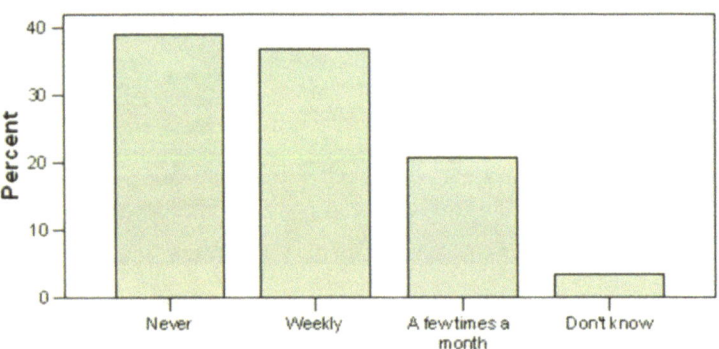

Fig. 86: Muslim reading Friday Bulletin

How often do you read the Friday Bulletin

It is important to note that these results referred to any form of television news since the survey did not specify Islamic Television or otherwise. Since no Muslim television existed

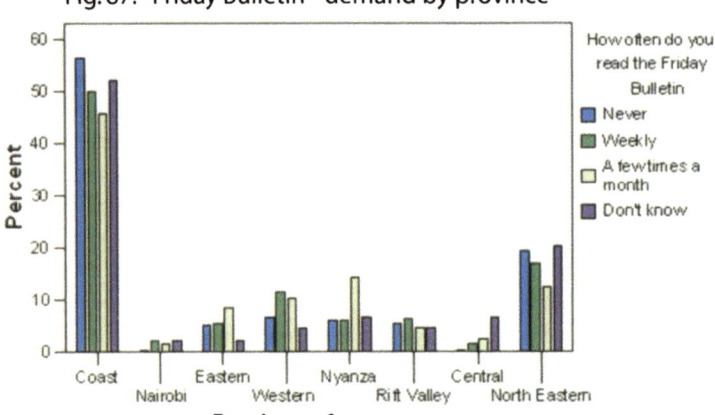

Fig. 87: Friday Bulletin - demand by province

Province of mosque

yet the responses show the dominance of general TV viewing amongst Kenyan Muslims. However, the television is not the only source for information favored by Muslims.

The Friday Bulletin

There is no Muslim daily paper as yet in Kenya, though Muslims frequently publish pamphlets that carry information for Muslims. Some of these pamphlets have developed as major sources of information that circulates and is consumed by Muslims.

The Friday Bulletin is a paper that has developed from a one page abridged Friday sermon to a weekly publication. During the survey a typical issue of the Friday Bulletin had between 6-10 pages Published and distributed for free from the Jamia Mosque in Nairobi, the Friday Bulletin appears to reach a wide Muslim audience.

Seventy five percent (75%) of Muslims read the weekly Friday Bulletin although some Muslims did not yet receive or read it.

The majority of Muslims from the Coast and North Eastern Province indicated they never had access to the Friday Bulletin. All Muslims in Nairobi, Central and Western Provinces read the Friday Bulletin. Generally some Muslims in Nyanza and Rift Valley Province have access to the Friday Bulletin, others did not.

Muslim women

Discussions on the position of women in society are highly emotive especially about the rights of women in Islamic societies. How Imams include this topic in their *khutba* shows some ambivalence.

A lot of discussion on the rights of women appears in the *khutba* of mosques from six out of the nine provinces. On the other hand, the topic is discussed 'just a little' in all provinces. Some few mosques in Coast, Eastern, Nyanza, Western, Rift Valley and North Eastern Provinces did not at all include discussions on the rights of women in the *khutba*. Reference was usually made to the fact that the Qu'ran dedicates a whole chapter to issues dealing with women.[8]

However, the way in which Imams address the issue of polygamy, inheritance and divorce is rather normative. Most Imams appear not to address these topics in relation to changes in society. In an attempt to gather sources in Kiswahili that address the rights of women, we only found one: Ustadh Harith Swaleh's, 'Mwanamke na Cheo Chake' (The Woman and her Status).

Generally accusations that Muslim society neglect and marginalize women are common. Muslims have sometimes found themselves having to defend Islam's position on women especially on aspects like personal laws, divorce, veil, the girl child and polygamy. This survey interrogated Muslims on aspects of religious practice in relation to Muslim women. It is common for Muslims to separate men and women in all public functions including prayers. This practice has been used as an example of the subordinate position that Muslims accord women. The survey indicates that over seventy percent (70%) of mosques adhere to the practice of separating men and women by having them pray in separate halls at the mosque.

Fig. 88: Imams speaking on rights of women

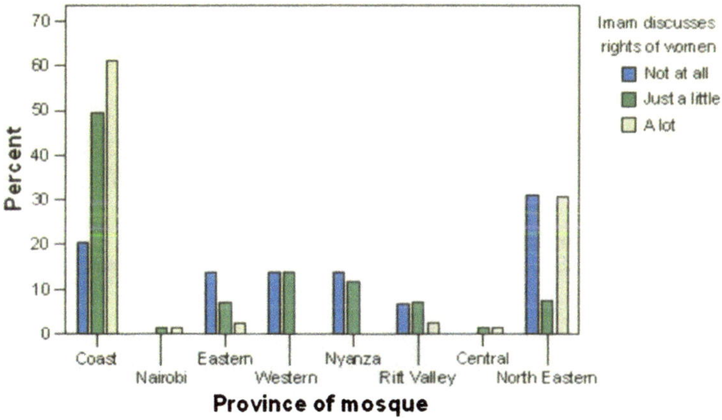

On leadership at the mosque, a significant number of mosques do not include women in the mosque committee. The majority of mosques, about eighty percent (80%) still did not want women or did not have women participants in the mosque committee.

When ana-

Fig. 89: Publication on Islam and woman

---

8) *This refers to Surat Nis'a (Qu'ran Chapter 4)*

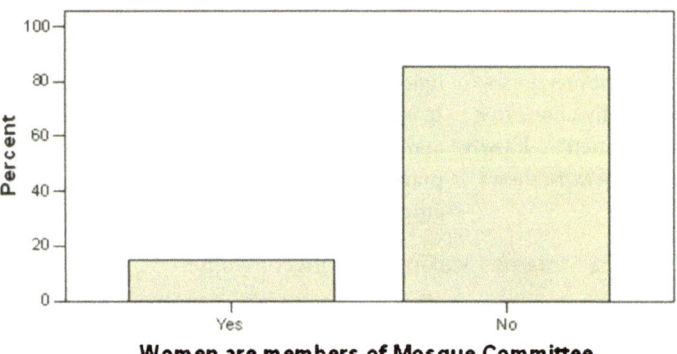

Fig. 90: Mosque including women in committee

lyzed further the data shows that Muslims will continue to exclude woman's participation in management of the mosque. Sixty five percent (65%) of respondents indicated their disapproval and were not ready to support the inclusion and participation of women in mosque committees.

Despite claims that women are the majority of voters' elective politics continue to be dominated by males in Kenya. Muslim women are particularly lacking in active political participation. There is only one Muslim woman member of parliament; she was not directly elected in the competitive politics but nominated by a political party. One Muslim woman had been vocal and active during the referendum supporting the eventual winning side, the Orange, which campaigned to oppose the draft constitution. A Muslim woman lawyer was also appointed to the Constitutional Review Committee and later rose to become its chair after the first chair resigned towards the end of the process. Abida Ali was later appointed to be judge of the Industrial Court making her the first Muslim woman to hold such a high office in Kenya since independence. By the time of writing the women's umbrella organization (maendeleo ya wanawake) had elected for the first time a Muslim woman to head the organization.

Despite such positive steps achieved by Muslim women the survey found that Muslim men disapprove of women's participation

Fig. 91: Muslim women at a public function

in elective politics. Only twenty eight percent (28%) of Muslims in this survey were in agreement about having women elected to political office.

Seventy two percent (72%) disagreed at having Muslim women elected to political office. From this high percentage, about thirty eight percent (38%) disagreed with the suggestion of allowing Muslim women to participate in elective politics while thirty four percent (34%) are very strongly opposed to having women elected to political office.

The survey included focused group discussions with women to identify the factors that hinder their development. We asked and wanted to find out the reasons responsible, for example, for the practice of ignoring women's potential in the public sphere.

We asked Muslims to respond by way of agreeing or disagreeing to the statement 'Muslim women are subjected to traditional laws and customs'. Responses to this query points to a divided Muslim opinion right at the heart of the matter. About forty eight percent (48%) strongly agreed that Muslim women were subjected to traditional laws and customs within the Muslim community. These customs are said to hinder women's potential.

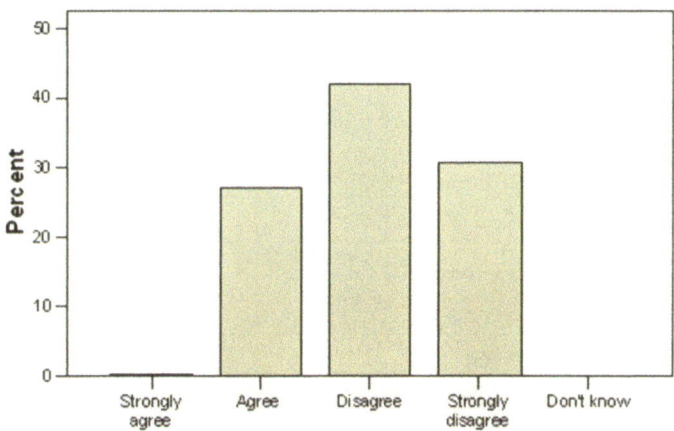

Fig. 92: Should Muslims men support Muslim women for elective political positions?

Fig. 93: Muslim women and customary practices

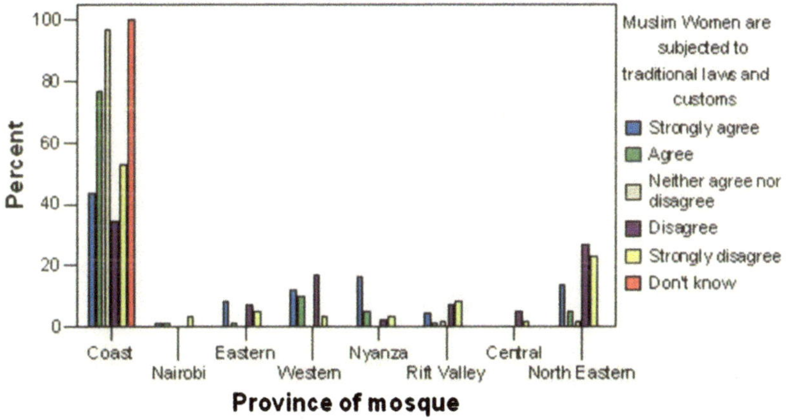

This meant that even where Islam allowed some women freedom and accorded them some rights, customary practice of such societies hinder even those rights accorded by religion. In Kwale District for example land ownership was an issue that was mentioned by women in several discussions. Although Islam allows women to inherit property it is common that land is usually inherited by the male heirs contrary to the religious requirement but in conformity to customary practices. In North Eastern Province Muslim women could not identify initiation rights for girls within Islamic teachings. However, the initiation rites continue to be practiced because society demands that 'young girls cannot just be left like that'.[9]

---

9) *Interview with Mama C in Mandera.*

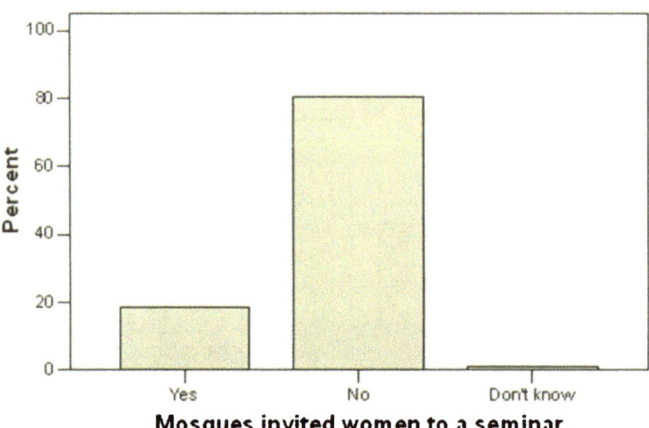

Fig. 94: Mosques inviting women to seminars

The majority of Muslims held the view that Muslim women were not subjected to traditional laws and customs. About twenty one percent (21%) of Muslims simply disagreed with the statement while thirty percent (30%) thought that the statement was entirely wrong and responded by strongly disagreeing that Muslim women were subjected to traditional laws and customs.

In the provinces the majority of Muslims in the Coast strongly disagreed with the statement that Muslim women were subjected to traditional laws and customs. A similar majority was also captured amongst Muslims from North Eastern Province. Nyanza Province was the only one which recorded a majority of Muslim who strongly agreed with the statement that Muslim women were subjected to traditional laws and customs.

Muslim women's lack of visibility in the public sphere was also reflected by how much mosques were ready and willing or had earlier organized or invited women's participation in its seminars. Seventy six percent (76%) of mosques had not made any effort to invite women to participate in seminars held at the mosque. Only twenty two percent (22%) had made an effort to invite women to attend seminars at the mosques. Lack of women's participation in educational gatherings at the mosque has a negative impact on Muslim society.

Generally, the sample contained Muslims disapproving of the practice of women participating in active politics. However, the extent to which such was disapproved of varied from one province to the other. For example, Muslims in North Eastern Province recorded the most disapproval towards Muslim women's participation in politics in Kenya. In the Coast Province fifty percent (50%) of Muslims agreed that Muslim women should be elected to political office compared to about forty two percent (42%) who strongly disagreed to the practice

Fig. 95: Young Muslim women at a public function

of encouraging women's participation in elective politics.

Social services

The survey shows that Muslim areas face a major shortage of social services. The ability of Muslims to provide social facilities including libraries, social halls, medical services and credit facilities is minimal. For example, the general trend amongst Muslims in Kenya was that their access to a library ranged from being very difficult to Muslims not having made an effort to look for a library in their living environments.

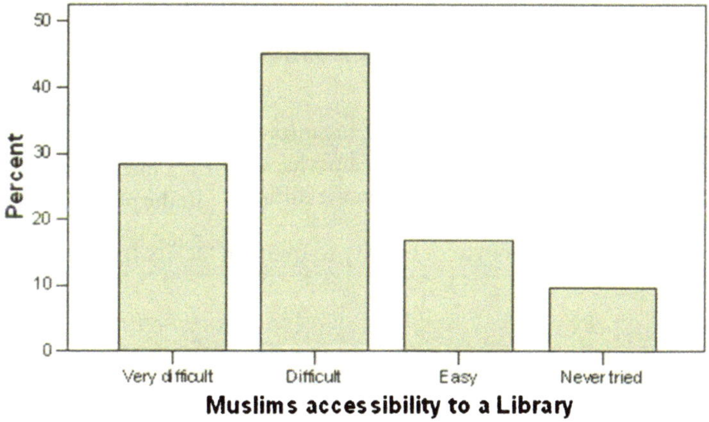

Sixty eight percent (68%) of Muslims either found it 'very difficult' or 'difficult' to find a library in their neighborhoods.

Out of the sixty eight percent (68%) who did not have access to a library thirty percent (30%) indicated that it was 'very difficult' and thirty eight percent (38%) responded that it was 'difficult' to access a library. Slightly above ten percent (10%) of Muslims were yet to make an effort to look for a library where they lived while fifteen percent (15%) found it easy to find a library.

Muslims in the Coast Province recorded the greatest difficulty, sixty percent (60%) of them said it was difficult to access a library. Fifty two percent (52%) of the total survey population who had not made an effort to look for a library were polled living in the Coast Province. In Nyanza the majority of Muslims lived in close proximity to a library, it was easy for them to access one.

Similarly Muslims experienced difficulties in locating a social hall where a public social function could be held. Most Muslims either found it very difficult or difficult to have access to a spacious facility where they could hold functions.

Fig. 96: Muslim access to library

Muslims accessibility to a Library

There are a few of such places. Those available were not easily accessible to Muslims. In Mombasa the Muslim Women Institute has a social hall along Digo road. However Muslims at the coast indicate that it is difficult to have access to such facilities. A small percentage, nineteen percent (19%), of Muslims in the Coast Province said it was easy to access a social hall nearby. A significant forty eighty (48%) of Muslims in this Province did not try to look for a social hall. Most Muslims in North Eastern Province also did not try to look for a social hall in their neighborhoods.

Muslims in Nyanza and Rift Valley Provinces enjoyed easy access to a social hall. Most respondent from Nairobi also indicated they had easy access to a social hall.

The provision of medical care is a major concern for not only the government but also

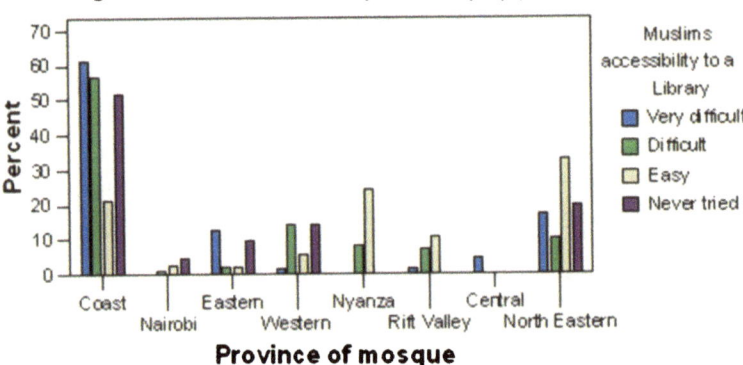

Fig. 97: Muslim accessibility to library by province

some Muslim non-governmental organizations. In the last decades medical facilities have become dilapidated. Kenyans found it difficult to access affordable medical care as state institutions implemented SAP, making it difficult for people to have access to improved health care.

Like other Kenyans Muslims were faced with the difficulty of inadequate medical facilities. The survey found that it was either very difficult or difficult for most Muslims to access a medical facility. Thirty eight percent (38%) of Muslims considered it extremely difficult for them to get access to a medical facility while 35% said it was difficult for them to visit a medical facility.

In the provinces the hardest hit of Muslims are those in the Coast Province. About fifty five percent (55%) of respondents in the Coast Province faced significant difficulties accessing health facilities compared to less than five percent (5%) in Nairobi, Eastern, Rift Valley and Central Province. The majority of Muslims in North Eastern Province also indicated that it was a serious difficulty for them to access a medical facility in the province. In Western, Nyanza and Rift Valley Provinces the majority of its Muslim populations indicated that it was easy for them to access a medical facility.

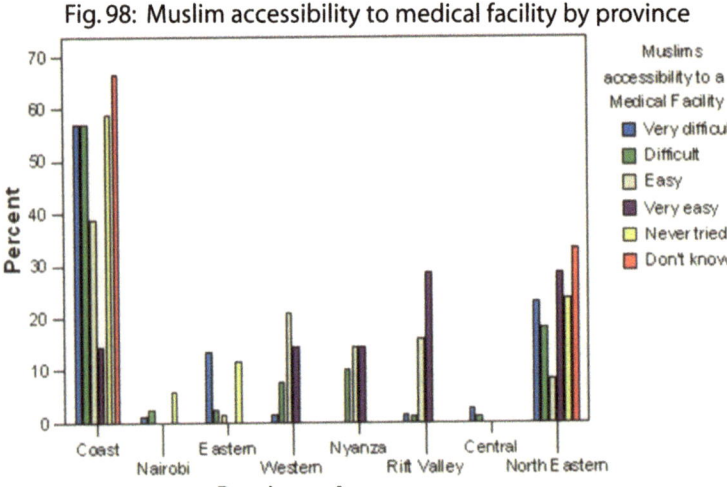

Fig. 98: Muslim accessibility to medical facility by province

Access to madrasa

The *madrasa*, an institution in which Muslims acquire knowledge on Islam, was perhaps the most easy to access for Muslims in comparison to other social amenities and needs. About seventy eight percent (78%) of the sample population of Muslim in Kenya experienced easy access to the *madrasa*.

Fig. 99: Muslim accessibility to madrasa

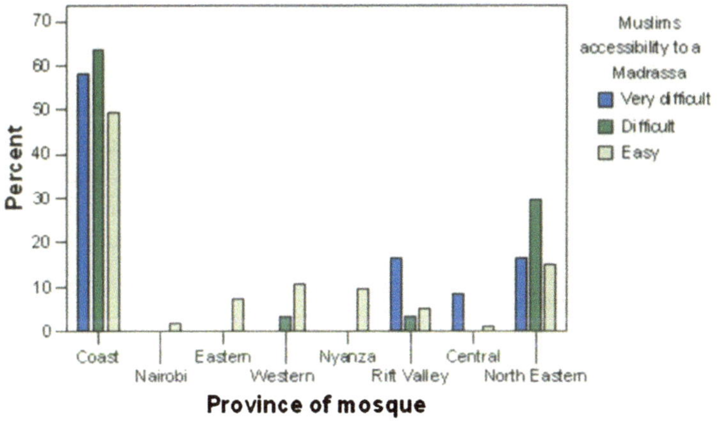

About 12% find it difficult to access the *madrasa* while the worst situation where it was very difficult to access a *madrasa* was experienced to by eight percent (8%) of the sample population of Muslims.

The results on how Muslims accessed the *madrasa* were rather surprising for the Coast Province where it appears that the demand for madrasa was stretched to the limits. Sixty five percent (65%) of the sample indicated that it was very difficult to have access to the *madrasa* while fifty eight percent (58%) of all those who responded that it was difficult to access *madrasa* were in the Coast Province. Only thirty eight percent (38%) responded by 'easy' access to the *madrasa* in the Coast Province.

This phenomenon is only explainable in relation to the high demand that could not be met for *madrasa* institutions. A similar situation was noticeable in North Eastern Province where demand for *madrasa* outstripped those available. Most Muslims in North Eastern Province were not adequately placed to find a *madrasa*. Nairobi Province provided a small percentage of the sample but all Muslims who were polled indicated that it was easy to access a *madrasa* in Nairobi. A similar situation was captured in Eastern and Nyanza Provinces where respondents indicated that they were in easy reach of *madrasa* education.

Credit facilities

The economic well-being of Muslims was determined on the basis of how well they could access credit to develop commerce and other economic activities. During the period of the survey a number of financial institutions had unveiled credit facilities that conformed to the Islamic monetary system. Non-interest lending had been established by major banking networks including Barclays (La Riba Account) and National Bank of Kenya.

However, the survey indicated it was still extremely difficult for Muslim to access credit. About seventy two percent (72%) of the sample survey said it was very difficult for them. There was about twenty percent (20%) of Muslims sampled who had not made an attempt to approach a financial institution intending to seek financial lending. A small per-

Fig. 100: La Riba Account

centage in the range of 5% of the samples returned the result that they had an easy access to credit.

In the Coast Province a majority of Muslims had easy access to credit while forty eight percent (48%) of Muslims in the province had difficulties accessing credit. About twenty five percent (25%) of Muslims polled from the Coast Province did not make any effort to seek credit in any financial institution. The figure for those who did not seek credit in North Eastern Province was similar to that which returned the result of easy access to credit.

A slightly lower percentage of Muslims in North Eastern Province had difficulties in accessing a credit facility.

Visits to mosques do not appear to be favored by politicians. The majority of mosques had not been visited by politicians either to solicit or influence worshippers' political views. About seventy percent (70%) of mosques indicated they had not been visited by politicians.

In the provinces Coast was leading in the percentage of mosques which had not been visited by politicians. In Nairobi all mosques indicated that they had not been visited by any politicians. However, in Eastern, West-

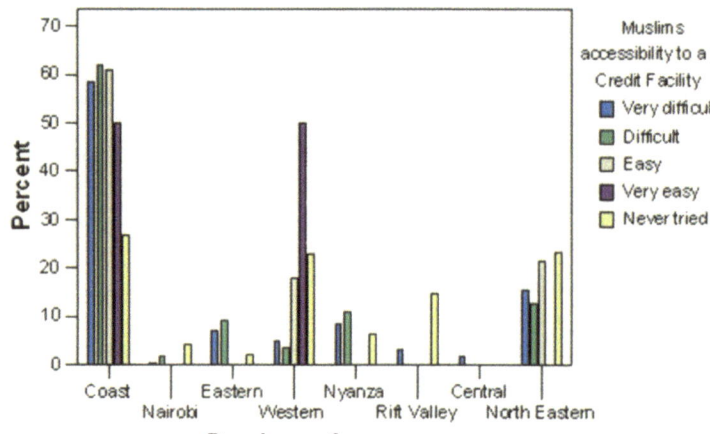

Fig.101: Muslim accessibility to credit by province

ern and Nyanza Provinces the majority of mosques had been visited by politicians.

Youth in the mosque

In 2005, the Chief Kadhi while speaking at the official opening of Imam Bukhari Mosque in Nairobi advised mosque committees in Kenya to encourage the participation of Muslim youth in the affairs of the mosques especially its management. The Chief Kadhi further advised mosque leaders to embrace program aimed at attracting the participation of the youth. He stressed that the functions of mosques should not be limited to *salat* (prayers) but include activities that will attract the youth and dissuade them away from mischief like drug abuse and crime. The survey asked how much the Muslim youth were included in the decision making organs of the mosques. The majority of mosques include youth in the management because they provide their representation in the mosque committee. Fifty seven percent (57.7%) of mosques have youth representatives in the committee while forty two percent (42%) did not include youth representation.

In the provinces, the Coast Province had the highest, sixty two percent (62%) of mosques indicating not to having youth represented in mosque committee. The majority of mosque in North Eastern also did not include youth representatives in their committees. Most mosques which included youth in their committees are located in Nyanza and Eastern Province.

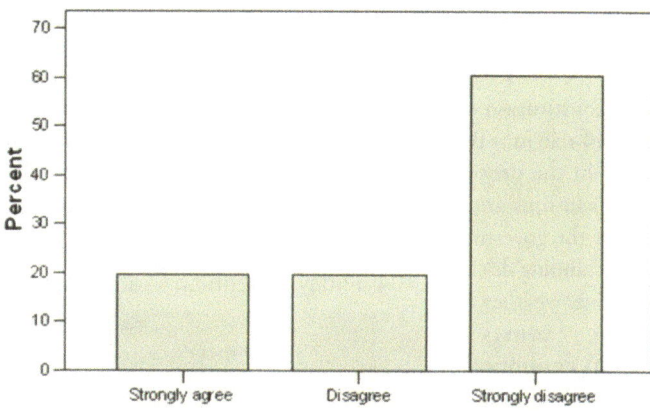

Fig. 102: Chief Kadhi's employer

Fig. 103: Friday Bulletin urging involvement of youth

SECTION SIX

Kadhi courts

The constitution of Kenya provides for freedom of religion. But in the recent past, especially in the process to review the constitution, Muslims and Christians and to a large extent the government remains engaged in a long-standing debate over whether *kadhi* courts should continue to be recognized in the new constitution. The *kadhi* courts have served Muslims since the early eighteen century. The constitution adopted during independence upheld their existence and the Kadhi's Court Act of 1967 established a venue for civil cases where especially Muslim personal matters of marriage, divorce, and succession were adjudicated. As far as the Constitution the *kadhi* courts are established and have jurisdiction where "all the parties profess the Muslim religion" in cases addressing "questions of Muslim law relating to personal status, marriage, divorce and inheritance". Articles 65 and 67 clarifies that *kadhi* courts are subordinate and they are supervised by the secular High Court. Constitutionally, the High Court can overrule decisions made in the *kadhi* courts in the event that the question at hand involves constitutional infringement.

During 2003 views were collected from Kenyans on what aspects of the Constitution require changes and reviews. In 2004, the National Constitutional Conference (Bomas) approved amongst other provisions freedom of worship (freedom of religion) and separation of church and state. Bomas also recommended that *kadhi* courts be enhanced and accorded an appellant status. In mid 2005 a coalition of Christian evangelical churches opposed vigorously and dangerously the *kadhi* courts on grounds that *kadhi* courts in the constitutions allegedly bestowed favors on the Muslim faithful. Muslim groups argue that other religious groups too could have their own courts in the constitution and in fact, the attorney general later included the provision of 'religious courts' in the draft constitution if only it would create a level playing ground amongst religious communities. With the efforts to write a new constitution defeated during the referendum the stalemate that ensued means the controversy over *kadhi* courts will continue to define Muslims attitudes towards the state but more important it will continue to reveal latent animosities between Muslims and Christians.

Since the process to review the constitution began in Kenya, the post of Kadhi has caused conflict between groups who support its inclusion in the Constitution and those opposed to it. The survey wanted to measure how much Muslims have information on Kadhis in Kenya. We began by finding out if Muslims were aware of who employs the Chief Kadhi by suggesting to Muslims that the Chief Kadhi was employed by a Muslim organization. Respondents to the survey showed that they were

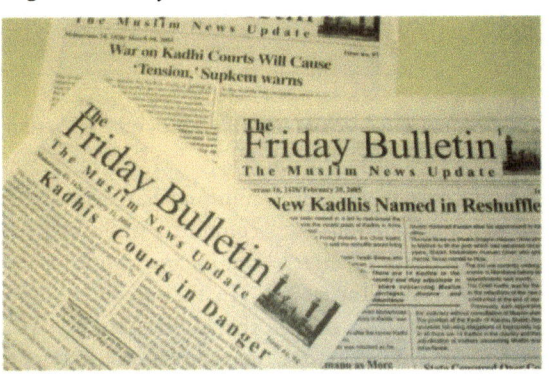

Fig. 104: Friday Bulletin on kadhi court

aware that the Chief Kadhi was not an employee of any Muslim organization.

The majority of respondents strongly disagreed with the statement that the Chief Kadhi was a salaried employee of a Muslim organization. About 18% of respondents thought there was some truth to the statement and strongly agreed with its proposition that the Chief Kadhi was employed by a Muslim organization while close to twenty percent (20%) of the survey population 'did not know' who employs the Chief Kadhi.

Muslims were particularly serious that the emotive matter of the inclusion of *kadhi* court in the constitution should not be debated by adherents of other religions. The majority of Muslims were of the opinion that the matter was internal to the Muslims who alone should decide on its fate in the Constitution.

While their inclusion in the Constitution was contested, *kadhi* courts appear to be popular amongst Muslims.

The survey indicated that almost eighty percent (80%) of respondents knew of a friend or member of their family who had visited the *kadhi* courts in the previous year (2005). The constitutional debate made Muslims more aware of the significance of the *kadhi* court but they nevertheless had prior knowledge of their existence and operations before the furor brought about by opposition to the 'entrenchment' of the court in the constitution. The survey found out that thirty percent (30%) of Muslims agreed not to have had adequate knowledge of the *kadhi* courts prior to the debate in the constitutional review process.

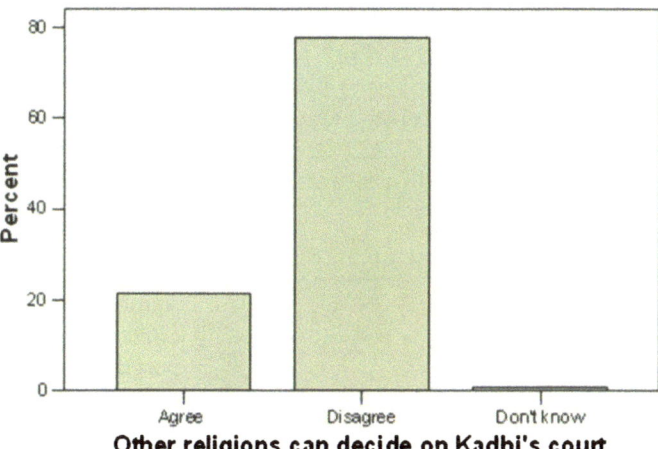

Fig. 105: Involvement of other religious communities on kadhi court dispute

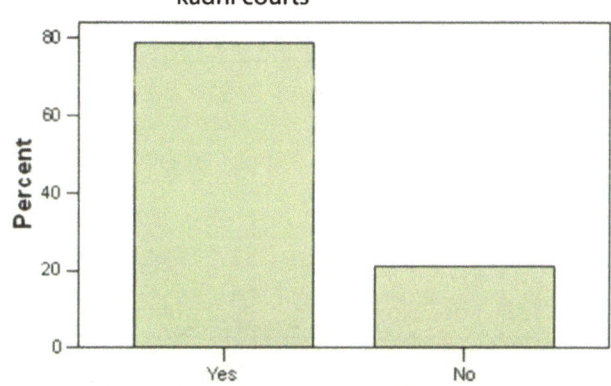

Fig. 106: Frequency at which Muslims visit kadhi courts

Fig. 107: Muslim urged to reject proposed constitution during referendum

Muslims realize that their minority status may not be an advantage in the event that a constitutional matter like the *kadhi* court is put to the vote. The likelihood that non-Muslims may use their numerical advantage as well as some drummed up anti-Muslims sentiments is real in Kenya. The manner in which debate on the century long *kadhi* court was conducted reveals a lot. Christian fundamentalist and evangelical groups rallied other Christians to condemn the courts as an attempt to introduce *shariah* laws in a 'Christian' country. Despite their relative minority status the majority of Muslims feel that they should demand the courts as their constitutional right and not as a favor by government or followers of other religions.

The survey found out that it was the feeling of a majority of Muslims that it is not a condition for them to support the government for them to be guaranteed state's support of the *kadhi* courts. About sixty eight percent (68%) of Muslims felt that *kadhi* courts were a right for Muslims and not a privilege, yet a significant fraction of twenty six percent (26%) felt that if need be for Muslims to support the government in return for guarantees on the *kadhi* courts, Muslims should not hesitate to do so.

Muslims and the West

The West is not a homogenous society but Muslims tend to perceive it as such especially in relation to positions taken by American on global politics. Some events, including the invasion of Iraq, the war in Afghanistan and the unresolved demand for the creation of the state of Palestine tend to influence Muslims' perception of the West. Muslims appear largely suspicious of the so called 'war on terror' which some Muslims believe is a means to target them for cultural profiling.

Sixty eight percent (68%) of Muslims interviewed strongly agreed that their perception of the West was influenced by the wars in Iraq and Afghanistan. Usually that percep-

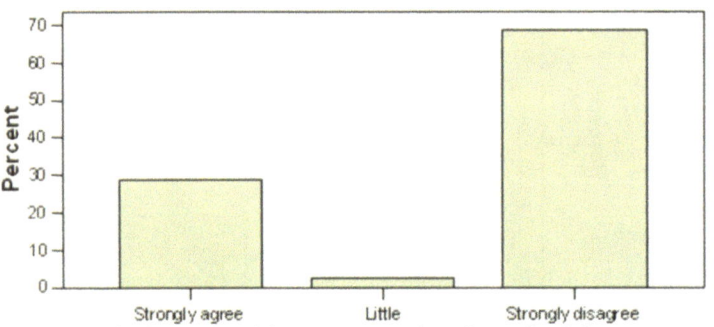

Fig. 108: Muslim to support government to ensure protection of kadhi courts

tion was a negative one. Twenty percent of respondents (20%) strongly disagreed to the suggestion that Muslims' perception of the West was influenced by the wars in Iraq and Afghanistan.

The majority of Muslims in the Coast Province indicated that the war had 'little' influence on their perception and attitudes towards the West. However, it is also true that most of the demonstrations against the invasion of Iraq were by Muslims in the Coast Province and Nairobi. In North Eastern Province the majority of Muslims strongly concurred that their perception of the West was largely influenced by the American invasion of Iraq and the war in Afghanistan.

Asked whether Muslims should engage with the West in order to influence its politics, Muslim opinion appears divided between those in favor of a positive engagement and those in favor of avoiding any dealing with the West. Sixty five percent (65%) wanted Muslims to influence politics in the West. Twenty three percent (23%) agreed 'very little' with the suggestion of Muslims' engaging with the West with the intention of influencing its politics.

If Muslims cannot influence politics in the West, will avoiding engaging with the West

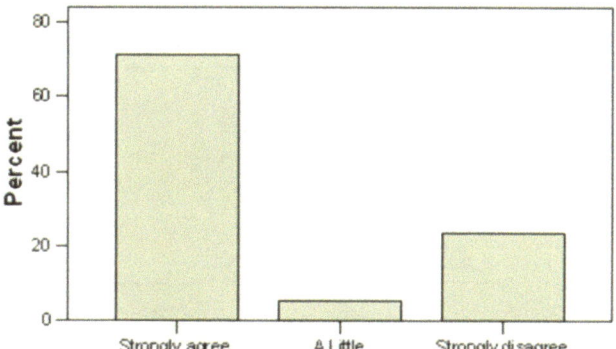

Fig. 109: Muslim opinion of West influenced by invasion of Iraq and Afghanistan

be a favorable idea amongst Muslims? Fifty five percent (55%) of respondents thought Muslims should avoid engaging with the West, while forty five percent (45%) strongly disagreed with the suggestion that Muslims should avoid interaction with the West.

In the Coast Province Muslims were divided right at the middle on the question whether they should engage with the West or not. Fifty three percent (53%) strongly agreed with the suggestion but forty seven percent (47%) were strongly opposed to engaging with the West. Similarly, the majority of Muslims in North Eastern Province do not prefer to engage with the West. Muslims who preferred to engage

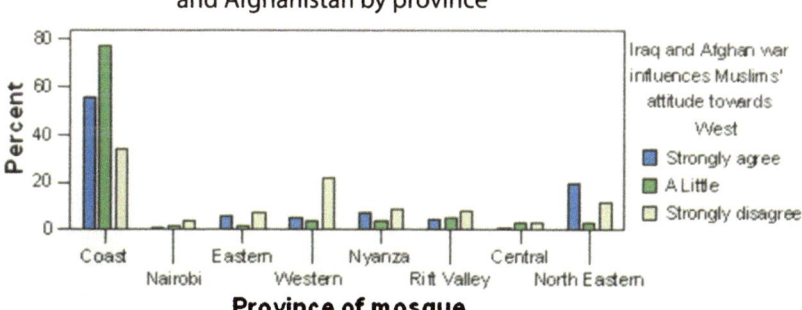

Fig. 110: Muslim opinion of West influenced by invasion of Iraq and Afghanistan by province

with the West were a majority in Rift Valley, Nyanza and Western Provinces.

Fig. 111: Muslim should influence politics in the West

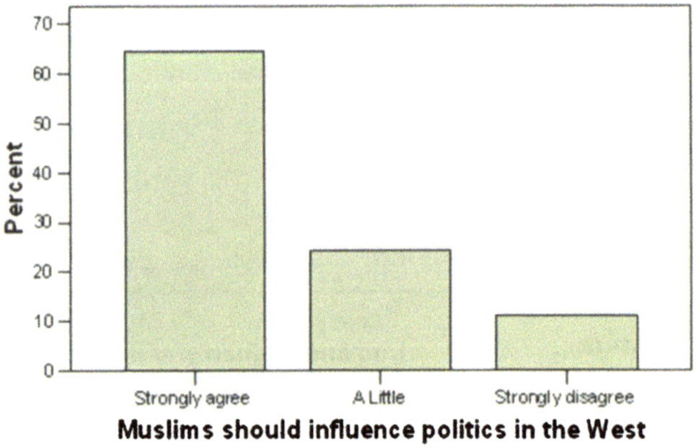

SECTION SEVEN

Muslim perspectives on economy and development

During the period of the survey Muslims' opinion of the economic conditions in Kenya was rated low. In fact forty one percent (41%) thought that the economic condition in the country was bad. Twenty one percent (21%) thought that economic conditions were good while slightly less than 20% thought economic performance was average. A small percentage of about 7% of Muslims polled were positive about the economic conditions in Kenya and thought prospects were very good.

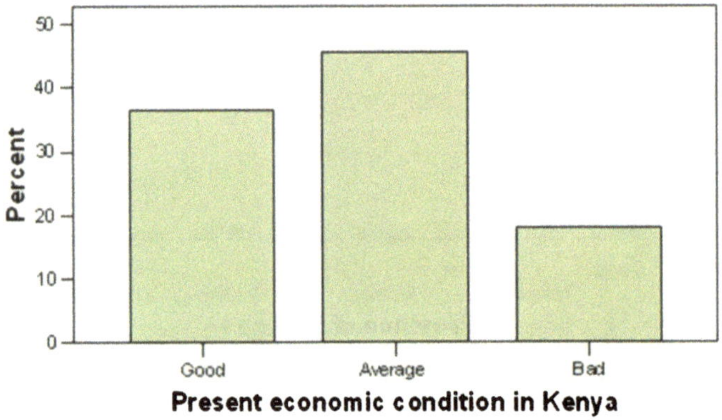

Muslims rated low economic conditions in Kenya, conditions which further exacerbated their poor living conditions. When asked to choose between a characterization of their living conditions from very good, good, average and bad, thirty eight percent (38%) thought their present living conditions were bad. About thirty two percent

Fig. 112: Muslim views of economic conditions in Kenya

(32%) of Muslims viewed their living conditions as good yet between four to five percent (4%-5%) thought they were doing very well in their present living conditions. Another twenty eight percent (28%) thought they were about average.

Muslims in the Coast Province appears to be the hardest hit by the poor present state of living conditions. About sixty one percent (61%) of Muslims in Coast Province said their present living conditions was bad. Similarly a large percentage of Muslims in North Eastern Province characterized their present living conditions as bad.

Muslims' comparison of the year (2006) to the previous (2005) years' economic conditions further fluctuates between positive and pessimistic.

Thirty eight percent (38%) of Muslims rated 2006 economic conditions in 2006 as remaining the same, about forty one percent (41%) thought 2006 was worse than 2005. Twenty four percent (24%) of Muslims thought the past year's economic conditions were better compared to the present (2006).

Muslims were hopeful about the future. Some forty percent (40%) thought their economic conditions would improve for the better. A small percentage, ten percent (10%) anticipated improvement of the economic conditions in the future. Compared to the previous year (2005), fifteen percent (15%) of Muslims thought that their economic conditions would remain the same but thirty percent (30%) expected to be badly off.

Fig. 113: Muslims present economic conditions

Present living condition in Kenya

In the provinces, Muslims' expectations of their future economic conditions varied. In Coast Province sixty eight percent (68%) expected that economic condition would improve to be 'much better'. About forty five percent (45%) thought next year's (2007) eco-

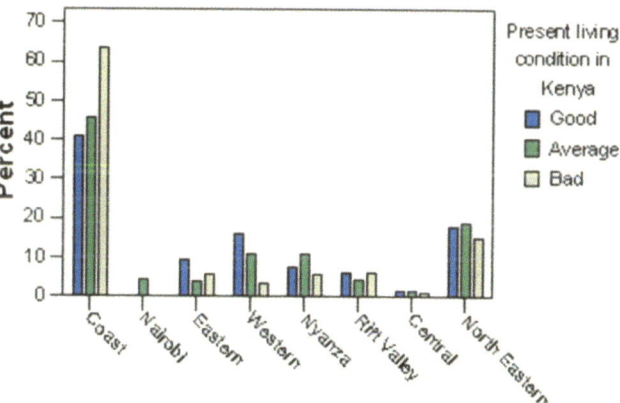

Fig. 114: Muslim living conditions by province

nomic conditions would be better for them. This is different in Nairobi.

Only two percent (2%) of Muslims in Nairobi expected better economic conditions. Muslims in Eastern Province recorded two choices for their expectations of economic conditions. A majority of Muslims, nineteen percent (19%) in Eastern Province complained that economic conditions would get worse in the future.

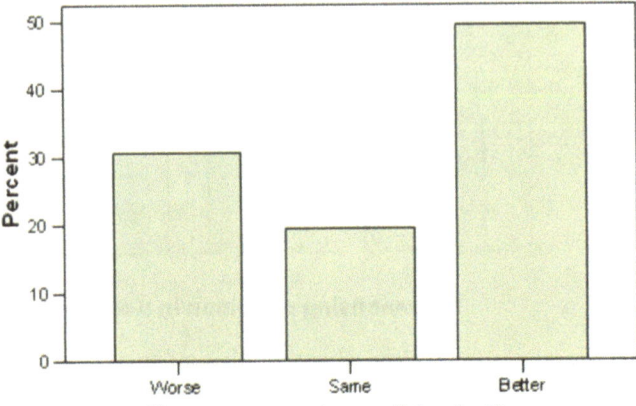

Fig. 115: Muslim expectation for future economic conditions

Muslims priorities for development

During the survey Muslims identified priority areas to which they wished the government and Muslim groups and other development agencies would give priority to enhance development.

Out of seven priority areas mentioned in the survey, education received the highest preference. About thirty percent (30%) of the survey population mentioned education. Sixteen percent (16%) was in favor of enhancing political participation amongst Muslims. Those who felt that unity amongst Muslims should be addressed amounted to sixteen percent (16%). Fourteen percent (14%) of Muslims wanted development agencies and the state to look into programs that tackle poverty in Muslim areas while unemployment was mentioned as a priority area by close to twelve percent (12%) of survey respondents. Health and drug abuse was considered significant by almost ten percent (10%) while less than four percent (4%) mentioned family counseling as a priority to enhance development in Muslim areas.

On the other hand, about thirty percent (30%) of Muslims in North Eastern Province

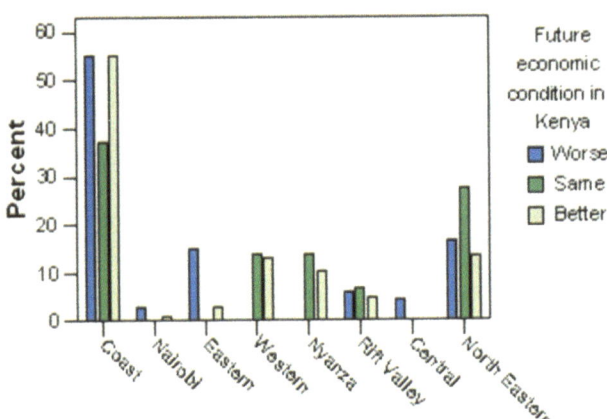

Fig. 116: Muslims expectations for future economic condition by province

thought their economic conditions would remain the same; about twenty five (25%) expected an improvement, while fifteen percent (15%) of Muslims in North Eastern Province expected their economic status to be better.

In the Coast Province Muslims comprising thirty eight percent (38%) wanted the government, Muslim development agencies and other civil society groups to prioritize economic empowerment and unemployment. Muslims who thought that education was important in order to enhance development comprised twenty two percent (22%) of the survey population.

Fifteen percent (15%) of Muslims in the Coast Province wanted health and drug abuse to be given priority, while another fifteen percent wanted Muslims to take an active role in politics as a way to enhance development. Ten percent (10%) preferred that Muslims insist on good leadership and Muslim unity to realize development. The fight against terrorism as a way to enhance development was given priority by four percent (4%) of the survey population in Coast Province.

In North Eastern Province thirty eight percent (38%) of Muslims preferred that economic empowerment, unemployment and poverty alleviation was given priority to enhance development amongst Muslims in the province. About twenty percent (20%) wanted Muslims to prioritize political participation and twenty percent (20%) wanted education to be given priority to enhance development. Eighteen percent (18%) of Muslims in North Eastern Province wanted health

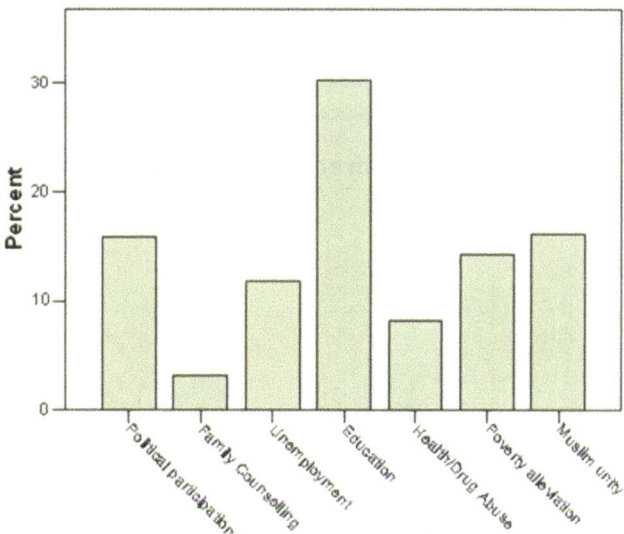

Fig. 117: Muslim priorities for development

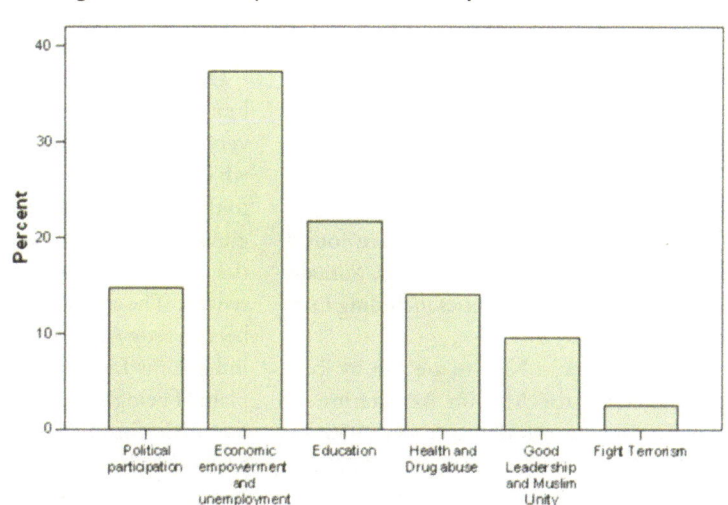

Fig. 118: Muslims priorities for development in Coast Province

Area 2 Preference for Muslims in the Coast Province to enhance development and drug abuse to be addressed in the development agenda.

Unlike other provinces Muslims in North Eastern Province had unique concern over religious consciousness and peace building. Two percent (2%) wanted religious consciousness to be addressed as a way to enhance development while the search for peace was mentioned by another two percent (2%) of Muslims in North Eastern Province.

Fig. 119: Muslim priorities for development in North Eastern Province

Area 3 Preferance for Muslims in North Eastern Province to enhance development

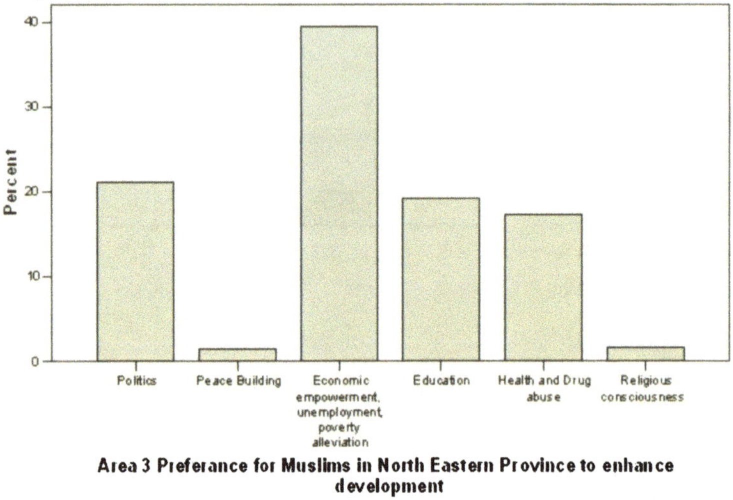

CASE STUDIES

In this section I will present selected narratives of case studies of areas included in the national survey.

Mosques in Nakuru

Nakuru District is in the Rift Valley Province. It is multi-ethnic and Muslims are found amongst Arabs, South East Asians, Somalis and local ethnic communities including Luo, Kikuyu and Luhya.

Muslim affairs in Nakuru are run by local organizations, the Muslim Association of Nakuru which was founded in the 1930s by Muslim railway workers from the Indian subcontinent. The Muslim Association of Nakuru is one of the most active Muslim groups. From its founding it began by engaging in the building of *madrasas* and mosques and established *wakf* to ensure continuity of these institutions.

Due to its development activities, the Muslim Association of Nakuru has always been in very good standing with the government which recognized their efforts. Membership to the association appeared restricted and eligible Muslims had to undergo vetting before they could be allowed to participate in its activities. The association has only 200 members, mostly Asian Muslims. It is common for indigenous Luo and Kikuyu people to complain of being excluded from the organization. Some Muslims from indigenous communities accuse Muslims of Asian origins of favoritism because they allow membership and participation in the association only to those Africans who did not criticize the Asian leaders. Muslims who have been excluded, especially African Muslims, have raised complains of being left out in the management of the organization and hence proclaim the leaders of the organization as self styled.

Since only a few Muslims participate in the elections of officials of the Muslims association those elected are usually accused of imposing their will up on the Muslim *ummah* of Nakuru. The association has assets: amongst them, a clinic, rentable property (houses), shopping complex, a parcel of land, library, and 15 mosques in Nakuru fall directly under the leadership of the association.

The association has also experienced ideological conflict between *salafi* oriented Muslims and the traditionalists (Wahhabi Islam against *tariqa*). During the period of this research the leaders of the association were thought of as being inclined towards *tariqa* Islam. Leaders of the association are usually accused of corruption, lack of transparency and accountability for not holding frequent elections in accordance to its constitution. During the period of the survey Muslims who felt aggrieved had lodged a court case to seek intervention.

The largest mosque in Nakuru is the Grand Jamia Mosque located in the centre of Nakuru town. Built in the 1930s this mosque one of the oldest in town. It is managed by the Nakuru Muslims Association. The mosque accommodates different views on religious practice. The *mawlid* is an important annual event at the mosque. Other controversial aspects of religious practice including the recitation of the *qunut*, or reciting the *bismillah*, loudly during prayers depend on the Imam. The mosque has an Imam and his assistant. The main Imam of the Grand Jamia is of Somali ethnic background and claimed to be associated with Wahhabi doctrines while the assistant Imam appears more favorable to the *tariqa* approach. It is common that the Imam will not recite *qunut* during *fajr* prayer but the assistant Imam would. Railway Mosque was built in the 1990s through assistance from the Nairobi based Young Muslim Association (YMA). It is managed by an elected committee, has a section for women and a *madrasa* in the compound. Bondeni (a part of the town) Mosque is another of the important mosques in Nakuru. The mosque was built through the efforts of local indigenous communities. Its tradition is associated with the *tariqa* and *mawlid* is an important annual event. Somali Mosque is relatively new in Nakuru having been built in the year 2000. Muslims from the Somali ethnic groups felt left out in the management and control of religious practice at the main mosque. They were particularly disappointed by the way worship was conducted at the Grand Jamia Mosque which did not conform to the strict Wahhabi inclined teachings. The Somali who were in favor of the Wahhabi teachings and practice opted to build their own mosque. The Somali mosque is therefore associated with the strict Wahhabi inclination. For example, saying the *bismillah* aloud during prayers is completely forbidden. Unlike other mosques, the Somali Mosque in Nakuru does not have a working committee and decisions at the mosque are said to be rather arbitrary. However, the mosque is one of the most progressive. It owns and manages a primary school that adapts an integrated school curriculum. The mosque has a section for women.

Noor Mosque is located in the middle class neighborhood, section 58 of Nakuru town. It was built in 1991 by a wealthy Muslim philanthropist in order to ease the difficulty Muslims were facing because of having to travel long distance to the centre of town to attend the *jumaah* prayers. Noor Mosque has an annual *mawlid* celebration and has a recently established committee which helps to run a *madrasa* and is responsible for the Imam's salary. Noor mosque is one of the few mosques where the Imam is housed in a descent property owned by the mosque. Shabab is another prominent mosque in Nakuru; this mosque takes the name of the living quarter in which it is situated. Shabab Mosque celebrates *mawlid*, has a section for women and a very successful and highly rated *madrasa* in Nakuru.

Mosques in Kisumu

Kisumu is a cosmopolitan city in Nyanza Province. Muslims comprise Somali, Arab (mostly Yemeni), and indigenous Luo people. There are two *aqidah* orientations in Kisumu. The Somali are mostly associated with the Wahhabi doctrines, while Yemeni Arabs and the indigenous Luo and some south east Asian (Indian) Muslims appear inclined to *tariqa* Islam.

Muslim leadership in Kisumu is often associated with the Kisumu Muslim Association a community based *awqaf* which practically runs and manages most of the mosques and other Islamic institutions in Kisumu. The association is well endowed with assets meant for the common good of all Muslims in Kisumu. The management of the association and its endowments is also one of the single most common sources of conflict amongst Muslims in Kisumu.

Amongst the most prominent mosques in Kisumu is the Grand Jamia Mosque which is under the management of the Muslim association. Constructed during 1909 with a holding capacity of two thousand worshippers this is one of the largest mosques. The mosque has a section for women and a *madrasa*. It also runs the Al-Mumin Primary School that adopts an integrated school curriculum.

The Railway Mosque is another of the important mosques in Kisumu. It was built in the 1990s and managed by the Kisumu Muslim Association (KMA). In 2004, the old mosque was demolished and a new modern structure put up with financial support from the International Islamic Relief Organization (IIRO) of Saudi Arabia. Through the support of IIRO, the Railway Mosque has a *madrasa*, a clinic and an orphanage. This mosque is dominated by Somali people and follows a strict Wahhabi interpretation of Islam. Rituals and practices associated with *tariqa* groups like the *mawlid* and *dhikr* are forbidden.

Manyatta Mosque in Kisumu is located in the Manyatta Arab Estate. It was built in the 1930s by Yemeni Arab traders who settled in Kisumu. Manyatta Mosque has been associated with *tariqa* traditions of *mawlid* and *dhikr* for a long time. However, times have changed and most of its *ratibs* have abandoned that tradition and have come under a strong Wahhabi influence. Shaykh Said, the octogenarian leader of the Yemeni Arabs narrates his personal experiences on changes and conviction. Shaykh Said claims to have memorized all the texts of the *mawlid* in the same way that people memorize the Qu'ran. However, he no longer considers the *mawlid* an important or relevant practice for Muslims. His main criticism of the *mawlid* is that it is an expensive practice that has impoverished Muslims. According to Shaykh Said, *mawlid* has remained a dominant practice amongst Muslims because of the lack of a reading culture in the community. Shaykh Said laments that Muslims do not read enough about their religion to be able to make independent reason. Lack of reading makes most Muslims dependent on the interpretations of Islam from others. He gives his own experiences that, once he exposed himself to a variety of Islamic literature he was able to make up his mind that *mawlid* has no significance any more. Shaykh Said hopes that as many more Muslims are exposed to reading Islamic text, the practice of people waiting to be told what is correct and wrong practice of Islam by others will stop and with it the many unnecessary controversies between Muslims.

Kaloleni Mosque in Kisumu is an old structure belonging to the local Luo Muslims. Estimated to have been built in the 1920's the Muslim community in Kaloleni is an example of changes from old to new. As the old mosque is dilapidated and almost falling down, the Muslims of Kaloleni are eagerly awaiting the completion of a new and modern mosque nearby. The benefactor constructing the new mosque with a capacity to hold three thousand worshippers is a local philanthropist and businessman. The ritualistic practice at the mosque is inclined to the *tariqa* and like the old mosque the new is expected to continue holding an annual *mawlid*.

Haji Issa is one of the most prominent Muslims in Kisumu. A long serving member of the KMA, Haji Issa was born in Nairobi around 1935 but grew up mostly in Kilimambogo in Thika. He started primary school at Thika in 1947 but did not progress beyond elementary level; he left and joined the *madrasa* after only one year of primary schooling. He rejoined school in 1952 and continued for the next four years and left to engage in business as a butcher and sisal farmer. Together with his father they moved to Muranga in 1957, where they continued with trade in livestock, traveling to collect animals from as far as Garba Tula and Isiolo. He moved to Kajiado in 1960 and continued on to live in Uganda from 1967 where he engaged in the Restaurant business for eight years. In 1974, he moved to Kisumu and was invited by local Muslims to join the KMA, under chairman, Sharif Ahmad Omar, with al Hajj Abulkadir. When Sharif Omar died in 1978, he became vice-chairman of KMA.

The 1970-1980s was a period of prosperity for the KMA which undertook development projects to improve on the quality of life of Muslims. KMA built secondary schools like the Muslim Mixed Secondary School, which was initially a Muslim girls secondary school. Other development projects undertaken by KMA included building of Kaloleni Primary School, construction of an office at the Jamia Grand Mosque, a mortuary at the mosque, shopping space, and the Imam's house. This calmness at the KMA was interrupted from early 2003 when the organization experienced wrangling over leadership and political conflicts. According to Haji Issa, the KMA had become a prosperous Muslim association and there was fear that some Muslims wanted to take control in order to mismanage the associations.

Manyatta Arab Mosque, Kisumu

According to its Imam, Sheikh Salim Said (68 years) the Manyatta Arab Mosque is one of the earliest mosques built in the Arab quarter in Kisumu. It was built by Arabs who traded in livestock. The Imam was born in Yemen and came to Kisumu at age 13. This mosque is considered as traditional and observes the *mawlid*. The Imam recalls with nostalgia how Muslims used to celebrate the *mawlid* together at the mosque to show Muslim brotherhood. The Imam is sad that new ideologies that are opposed to the *mawlid* rituals have been the cause for divisions amongst once peaceful Muslim community. In Kisumu, claims that the *mawlid* is *bid'a* (innovation) are propagated by ulama mostly from the Somali and Swahili groups.

Mosques of Mumias Town

Mumias town is located in Western Province, ninety kilometers from Kisumu town. Mumias division comprises six locations. Because of the central location of Mumias it was selected as a focus area of the survey in Western Province. The Muslim population of Mumias comprises the majority indigenous

Luhya ethnic group, Arabs, Somali and Nubians. It is recalled that Islam was introduced into Mumias by one Sharif Omar al Mahdaly in the third decade of the nineteenth century. Sharif Abdalla al Mahdaly and his family were itinerant traders in hides and skins from Tanga who institutionalized Islam in Mumias by converting the local ruler, Nabongo Mumia to Islam and thereby most of his Wanga ethnic group followed. It is also narrated that Sharif Omar Abdalla institutionalized the *mawlid* in Mumias which played a significant role in the Islamization process. Islam was attractive in Mumias thanks to the *mawlid* started in Mumias and developed a network as far as Uganda. *Mawlid* played a significant role in the process of Islamization and the spread of Islam in western Kenya. Sharif Umar, credited with having played a significant role in the islamization of Mumias died in Mumias and was buried in Kisumu. An annual *ziyara* to visit his tomb is held in Kisumu. Sharif Umar's legacy is continued by his grand son Sayyid Hassan, who is the Chairman of the SUPKEM at Mumias.

In Mumias it is not difficult for one to be struck by the presence and vibrancy of Islam from the imposing presence of the Mumias Grand Jamia Mosque located at the centre of town. This mosque was first built in 1838, was renovated in 1947 and 1990 through the efforts of the local community. The mosque has a section for women and runs a *madrasa* nearby. The Grand Jamia Mosque of Mumias is run by a committee of elected members. During the period of the survey the leader of the management committee was Mr. Ismail Muchelule, a businessman, elected council representative and a Director of MUMCO (Mumias Muslim Community Project). The MUMCO manages a clinic and has offices and social hall which it hires to provide financial support for its community support programs. MUMCO works towards improving the welfare of the Muslim community in Mumias. The Grand Jamia Mosque in Mumias has a richly endowed *wakf* fund from which it is able to meet financial obligations including paying salaries for Imam and *madrasa* teachers. Because of its central location and significance in the community the mosque is not associated with any particular *akidah*. The *mawlid* is celebrated annual, *bismillah* can be pronounced aloud during prayers, and possibilities for a congregational dua (supplication) are admitted. As a central mosque, the Grand Mosque has created a network of other mosques that are managed through here. Some of the mosques included in the network of the Grand Jamia Mosque of Mumias are discussed below.

Elkama Mosque was built around the 1980's through the foresight of Mr. Muchelule the chairman of the Grand Jamia Mosque. It is a small mosque, does not hold *jumaah* prayers, has no *madrasa* and *mawlid* is never held at this mosque. It has a committee which is appointed through its network at the Grand Jamia Mosque. Almost every aspect of the Elkama Mosque is associated with the Grand Jamia Mosque.

Lukoye Mosque is located just one thousand meters from the Grand Jamia Mosque on the road to Bungoma. It was built in the 1970's on land belonging to the *wakf* of the family of Mzee Akidah. The Lukoye Mosque is regarded by most people in Mumias as following an anti-*mawlid* ideology. It's also referred to as the centre of *salafi* teachings. However, its Imam is a young graduate of the College of Islamic Studies in Kisauni which is regarded as the centre of Wahhabi influence in Kenya.

Ekore Mosque is located on the road to Kakamega. It was constructed in the year 2000 by the local community. It is a Friday mosque with a strong tradition of holding the *mawlid*. Because it forms part of the network of the Grand Jamia Mosque, it does not hold eid prayers which are usually held at the Grand Jamia Mosque.

Shibale Mosque is another one in the network of the Grand Jamia Mosque. It was built in the 1980's. Located in the industrial areas, it caters mostly for the spiritual needs of factory workers. Because the industrial area was surrounded by residential areas the local Muslim community built this mosque and a nearby *madrasa* to ease the distance which people had to travel to the Grand Jamia Mosque. It has a section for women; it celebrates the *mawlid* and has a *wakf* whose resources are used to run mosque affairs.

Sheikh Khalifa Mosque, Lukoye Mumias was constructed in 1991 with financial assistance from a Kuwaiti donor. Activities like prize giving are held at the mosque annually *mawlid* is usually not held at the mosque since this ceremony is usually held at the Jamia Grand Mosque, *ratibs* at the mosque consider themselves to be *ahl-al sunna* that is they are not of the Wahhabi persuasions. There are no disputes reported on *ibadat* or rituals. The mosque has a committee chaired by a prominent businessman, the mosque has no *wakf* and occasionally *ratibs* are asked to contribute towards upkeep for the Imam. This mosque enjoys cordial relations with other mosques especially the Grand Jamia Mosque at Mumias. It was a practice sometimes back for the Grand Jamia Mosque to extend financial assistance to other mosques in Mumias, due to financial hardship the Grand Jamia mosque is unable to meet this anymore. The problems identified by the imam of Lukoye Mosque include lack of funds especially to pay the Imam's salary.

Tanwir Da'awa Women's Group Nakuru

This is a Muslim women group and CBO (community based organization) which was started in 1977. It incorporates a variety of activities and networks with other Muslim women groups in Nairobi and Mombasa in programs that sensitize Muslim women on their rights. Being the only women's group in Nakuru, it is forced to get itself involved in many other activities including *da'awa* and propagation of Islam. It also runs an orphanage and assists needy families with education by occasionally helping with paying school fees.

Habiba Mohamed Shaaban, its chairlady says the objectives of the group include improving the religious and social well-being of Muslims in Nakuru; care for AIDS orphans, educating the Muslim girl child and initiating income generating activities. Some of the activities initiated to raise funds to meet the cost of its programs include selling of lesos (khanga), agricultural commodities like coconut, groundnuts, and simsim; trading in spices including pilau mix. Members of the group contribute a monthly fee of 300 shillings. The women's group interacts with young Muslim boys and girls and gains their confidence so these young lads can reveal their problems which are later addressed by the women groups; another women's group that participates in this venture is the Ansar Women Group.

Conflicts at Mlango wa Papa Mosque

During the period of the survey a dispute had occurred at Mlango wa Papa Mosque in old town Mombasa. I discuss the nature of this dispute as an example of what happens in some mosques. Mlango wa Papa Mosque is one of the oldest mosques in Mombasa. It is situated in the Kuze quarters of Mombasa. Its *ratibs* include influential families and individuals in Mombasa. Mlango wa Papa Mosque can easily be termed *msikiti wa kimombasa* a typical Mombasa like mosque. It has a long history having been constructed around the sixteenth century by Arab immigrants. By the time of the survey the mosque was managed by a committee although its ownership lies with the Wakf Commission of Kenya. *Ratibs* at Mlango wa Papa Mosque can be said to entertain different religious rituals and all orientations and *akidah* were welcome. It *darsa* were patronized by scholars thought to have Wahhabi inclinations. *Mawlid* was a common ritual in the mosque's calendar and Muslims with *tariqa* felt at home. The mosque, because of its acceptance of all kinds of views, was the bastion of religious tolerance in Mombasa. But times have changed and Mlango wa Papa Mosque has had to bear the brunt of its historical tolerance as new controversies over ownership and *akidah* are experienced. The controversies at Mlango wa Papa are based on attempts by some people to control and exercise influence on how and what rituals will take place, which *alim* can deliver *darsa* and what topics can be discussed during the *darsa*. For example a young man C, who has been Imam at the mosque and gave *darsa* for a period of five years, was suddenly given instructions by some influential Muslim D on what topic to discuss. Even though the young Imam C complied with such demands he was forbidden to give *darsa* at the mosque by the influential Muslim D. Because the young Imam was of different racial identity from the influential Muslim D, the dispute at Mlango wa Papa acquired racial connotations. In 2004 the old building was pulled down and a new mosque was built; an attempt to take control over the new mosque polarized the community. In 2005 the new mosque was ready and before it could be used for worship, another conflict over its ownership emerged when the Wakf Commissioners advertised and invited applicants for the post of Imam. A candidate associated with the influential person D was appointed as Imam. The Wakf Commission has also registered a dispute in the court versus the group associated with the influential Muslim D, claiming ownership and the right to decide how affairs at the Mlango wa Papa Road Mosque can be run.

Bibliography

Bakari, Mohamed, and S. Yahya, eds. 1995. *Islam in Kenya*. Nairobi.

Berg, Fred J and B. J. Walter. 1968. "Mosques, population and urban development in Mombasa". In *Hadith 1*, ed. Bethwell A. Ogot. Nairobi. Pp. 47-100.

Constantin, Francois. 1993. "Leadership, Muslim Identities and East African Politics: Tradition, Bureaucratization and Communication." In Louis Brenner, ed. *Muslim Identity and Social Change in Sub-Saharan Africa*. London; Hurst; Pp. 36-58.

Constantin, Francois. 1995. "Muslims and Politics: Attempts to Create Muslim National Organizations in Tanzania, Uganda and Kenya." In H.B. Hansen, Michael Twaddle. Eds. *Religion and Politics in East Africa: The Period since Independence*. London; James Curry; Pp. 19-31.

Kresse, Kai. 2006. "Debating maulidi: Ambiguities and Transformations of Muslim Identity along the Kenya Swahili Coast." In Roman Loimeier, Rüdiger Seesemann, eds. *The Global World of the Swahili*. Berlin.

Kamrava, Mehran, ed. 2006. *The New Voices of Islam. Reforming Politics and Modernity*. London.

Metcalf, Barbara. 2004. *Islamic Contestations: Essays on Muslims in India and Pakistan*. Oxford.

Mwakimako, Hassan, 2007. "Christian-Muslim Relations in Kenya: A Catalogue of Events and Meanings." *Journal Islam and Christian Muslim Relations. Vol. 18 No. 2. April 2007*. pp. 287-307.

Oded, Arye. 1996. "Islamic extremism in Kenya: the rise and fall of Sheikh Khalid Balala", *Journal of Religion in Africa* 26: pp. 406-15.

Oded, Arye. 2000. *Islam and Politics in Kenya*. London.

Loimeier, Roman and R. Seesemann, eds. 2006. *The Global World of the Swahili*. Berlin.

Zaman, Muhammad Qasim. 2002. *The Ulama in Contemporary Islam: Custodian of Change*. Princeton and Oxford.

Bei Fragen zur Produktsicherheit wenden Sie sich bitte an:
If you have any questions regarding product safety,
please contact:

Walter de Gruyter GmbH
Genthiner Straße 13
10785 Berlin
productsafety@degruyterbrill.com